Doing
Psychology
Experiments

Sharon Sanborn 832-2678

Roger E. Kirk, Consulting Editor

EXPLORING STATISTICS: AN INTRODUCTION FOR PSYCHOLOGY AND
EDUCATION
Sarah M. Dinham, *The University of Arizona*

METHODS IN THE STUDY OF HUMAN BEHAVIOR
Vernon Ellingstad, *The University of South Dakota*
Norman W. Heimstra, *The University of South Dakota*

AN INTRODUCTION TO STATISTICAL METHODS IN THE BEHAVIORAL
SCIENCES
Freeman F. Elzey, *San Francisco State University*

EXPERIMENTAL DESIGN: PROCEDURES FOR THE BEHAVIORAL SCIENCES
Roger E. Kirk, *Baylor University*

INTRODUCTORY STATISTICS
Roger E. Kirk, *Baylor University*

STATISTICAL ISSUES: A READER FOR THE BEHAVIORAL SCIENCES
Roger E. Kirk, *Baylor University*

THE PRACTICAL STATISTICIAN: SIMPLIFIED HANDBOOK OF STATISTICS
Marigold Linton, *The University of Utah*
Philip S. Gallo, Jr., *San Diego State University*

NONPARAMETRIC AND DISTRIBUTION-FREE METHODS FOR THE SOCIAL
SCIENCES
Leonard A. Marascuilo, *University of California, Berkeley*
Maryellen McSweeney, *Michigan State University*

DOING PSYCHOLOGY EXPERIMENTS
David W. Martin, *New Mexico State University*

BASIC STATISTICS: TALES OF DISTRIBUTIONS
Chris Spatz, *Hendrix College*
James O. Johnston, *University of Arkansas at Monticello*

MULTIVARIATE ANALYSIS WITH APPLICATIONS IN EDUCATION AND
PSYCHOLOGY
Neil H. Timm, *University of Pittsburgh*

Doing Psychology Experiments

David W. Martin

New Mexico State University

Brooks/Cole Publishing Company
Monterey, California

A Division of Wadsworth Publishing Company, Inc.

This book is dedicated to:

My father, Daniel W. Martin, who taught me logical thinking,

My high school teacher Doris Mitchell, who showed me that teachers can care,

My undergraduate professor Harve E. Rawson, who introduced me to psychology,

My graduate professor the late George E. Briggs, who best demonstrated experimental rigor,

And all of my students, from whom I am continually learning to teach.

Printed in the United States of America

10 9 8 7 6 5 4

Library of Congress Cataloging in Publication Data

Martin, David W   1943–
   Doing psychology experiments.

   Includes index.
   1. Psychology, Experimental. I. Title.
BF181.M315   150'.7'24   77-4183
ISBN 0-8185-0230-4

Manuscript Editor: *Adrienne Harris*
Production Editor: *Micky Lawler*
Interior Design: *Laurie Cook*
Cover Design: *Jamie S. Brooks*
Illustrations: *Kevin East*

Preface

I didn't mean to write this book. I simply needed a text for my experimental psychology course. After I persistently complained to publishers' representatives that none of their available texts matched my needs, the fine folks at Brooks/Cole finally tried to placate me by sending me prospective texts to review. When I panned the fourth or fifth text they sent me, the editors politely requested that I "put up or shut up." Since my personality is constitutionally unsuited to the latter request, you are reading the product of the former.

The texts available at that time fell into three general categories, none of which reflected the emphasis of my course. In Category 1 were content-oriented texts giving a limited coverage to a wide range of experimental topics, such as learning and perception. Category 2 consisted of texts that emphasized statistics mixed with a little basic design. The texts in Category 3 attempted to teach the more advanced student some of the specialized methodological techniques of subareas such as psychophysics, psychophysiology, and learning. The text I needed (and I have since learned that many others have the same need) was one that would provide just enough information so that a student with no experimental background could design, execute, and report a simple psychological experiment. I hope that this book fulfills these goals.

Students new to experimentation typically have some basic practical questions: Where can I get an idea for an experiment? How can I find out what's already been done? How do I write an experimental report? Not until later in their careers do they become concerned with the more sophisticated techniques discussed in many standard methods texts.

Besides dealing with some of these basic practical questions, this book is unique in several other ways. For example, it has a chapter on the ethics of science as well as the ethics of subject treatment. For too long we have assumed that while we are teaching experimental techniques, the values of science will mysteriously rub off on our students. Chapter 5 discusses many of the typical ethical questions that confront new experimenters.

I have also attempted to write *Doing Psychology Experiments* in a friendly style. While those who teach psychology have finally admitted that introductory texts need not be written in a pedantic style, we still seem to be unwilling to write about the interesting material of our more advanced courses in an interesting way. Hopefully this text will be a forerunner of a number of less formal advanced texts.

I am indebted to a number of people and institutions for their financial, professional, and moral support. New Mexico State University allowed me to spend a sabbatical leave writing the book. The University of Oregon and Michael I. Posner in particular provided me with an office and friendly encouragement when my creativity waned. At Brooks/Cole (the friendliest publisher around), Bill Hicks had the courage to write down the first table of contents on a cocktail napkin. (It looked so good I had to go ahead with the project.) Roger E. Kirk provided compulsive, but not scathing, criticism of each thought in the book. He helped me keep a balance between informality and precision. Other reviewers of the manuscript were S. Joyce Brotsky of California State University at Northridge, B. R. Hergenhahn of Hamline University, and Daniel Lordahl of Brock University. I am also grateful to Adrienne Harris, my manuscript editor, Micky Lawler, my production editor, and Kevin East, who did the cartoons and technical illustrations. Finally, my thanks go to those who do the real work: my typists, Linda Nathan at the University of Oregon and Carolyn Fowler at New Mexico State University.

David W. Martin

Contents

How to Make Orderly Observations

Scientists, philosophers, theologians, alchemists, and psychologists are alike in at least one respect: they think. There are enormous differences among them in the ways that they employ thought; but the goal of their thoughts is strongly similar: to understand man and the universe in which he evolved.*

Psychologists go about their business much like scientists in other scientific fields. In their search for an understanding of human behavior, psychologists attempt to (1) establish relationships between circumstances and behavior and (2) fit these relationships into an orderly body of knowledge. In this book we will deal primarily with the first activity, although we will touch on the second activity in the final two chapters.

What kind of a relationship is acceptable to us as scientists? When we can demonstrate that one event is related to a second event in some predictable way, then we have a statement that will fit into the scientific body of knowledge. At least one of these events must be a measurable behavior. Here we can make a distinction among the sciences. The behavior of major concern to us as psychologists is human behavior (and sometimes animal behavior). And this is where we run into one of our first problems—a problem that haunts psychologists but not physical scientists. Humans are variable. We humans often cannot repeat a response precisely even if we wish to, and in some cases we may not wish to. In terms of variability, then, physical scientists typically have it easier than psychologists.

A physicist measuring the coefficient of friction for a wooden block might measure the time it takes the block to slide down an inclined plane. While the times might vary from trial to trial, such variability would be relatively small. The physicist would not be making too great an error to consider the variability a minor nuisance and eliminate it by taking the average of several trials. However, a psychologist who wants to measure the time it takes a human to press a button in response to a

*Monte, C. F. *Psychology's scientific endeavor.* New York: Praeger, 1975.

light would be making a considerably greater error by ignoring human variability. Although it is unlikely that our physicist's block will be a little slow on certain trials because it had its mind on other things, or wasn't ready, or was blinking or asleep, it is certainly possible for a human subject to experience these and many other problems.

In addition to variability among trials, variability among human subjects must also be taken into account by psychologists. Our physicist could construct another block of the same size, weight, and surface finish as the original and repeat the experiment. The psychologist, however, cannot recreate human subjects. Humans seldom have exactly the same genetic background (identical twins being an exception), and they never have exactly the same environmental background. For this reason it would be typical to find that, in responding to the light, one subject's fastest response is considerably slower than another subject's slowest response. Thus, as psychologists we have to deal not only with one person's variability from trial to trial but also with the variability among humans.*

---

*You can see why some psychologists decide to use animals as subjects. Whereas psychologists can breed animals with similar genetic characteristics and rear them in similar boxes, it would be frowned upon if they tried to do the same thing with humans. Your friends may say "All men are animals" or "All women are alike," but don't believe them!

One way to handle variability is to use statistical techniques. Many psychology students learn to do this by taking a statistics class early in their course work. Since this is not a statistics text, we will ignore most of the statistical solutions, although later in the book we will touch on the topic when we talk about interpreting the results of your experiments. A second way to handle variability is to control it as much as possible in the design of your research. This book is written to help you do good research, which is a simple way of saying "Know where the variability is, and be able to account for it."

THE EXPERIMENTAL METHOD

We as scientists establish relationships between events, but these events are not always behaviors. In fact, when we do an experiment, or use the *experimental method,* the relationship of interest is between a set of circumstances and a behavior. A physicist wants to know the time it takes a block to slide down a plane when the plane is at a particular angle, with a particular surface, and at a particular temperature. A psychologist wants to know the time it takes a person to press a button when the light is a particular intensity, a particular color, and in a particular place. Both scientists are attempting to establish relationships between a set of circumstances and a behavior. These relationships are scientific facts, the building blocks with which we build our science.

Unfortunately, designing an experiment to establish such a relationship is not always easy. Ideally, we would like to specify exhaustively and precisely a particular set of circumstances and then measure all of the behaviors taking place under those circumstances. We could then say that, whenever this set of circumstances recurred, the same behaviors would result. However, if we could list *all* of the circumstances, we would have a unique set. In our reaction-time experiment we would list not only the intensity and color of the light but also the temperature and humidity of the room, who the experimenter was, who the subjects were, what their ages were, how much sleep each had had the night before, what they had eaten for lunch, and so on. In other words, we would have a unique set of circumstances that would never be repeated.

Thus, we are caught in a dilemma. On the one hand, we want to build our science on statements of precise relationships between circumstances and behaviors. On the other hand, if we can do this, we end up with an infinite number of statements, one for each unique set of circumstances. We would never be able to predict behavior from circumstances, since we would not have seen those particular circumstances before. How do we resolve this paradox?

Figure 1-1 diagrams the situation. The lines on the left represent the components of a unique set of circumstances. The lines on the right represent the potential behaviors that could be measured (such as speed of response, strength of response, brain-wave activity, and blood pressure). Both of these lists are infinitely long. The arrow indicates the possibility of a relationship between the circumstances and the behaviors.

Circumstances   Behaviors

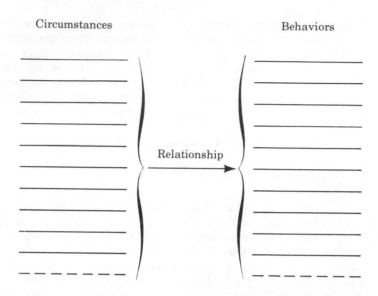

Figure 1–1.   A diagram representing the attempt by scientists to establish a relationship between a set of circumstances and measurable behaviors.

In order to resolve this paradox, scientists have had to make a compromise. They have chosen to specify only a general set of circumstances rather than every possible component of a unique combination of circumstances.

VARIABLES

Independent Variables

At least one circumstance is of major interest in an experiment (for example, light intensity in a reaction-time experiment). We call this circumstance an *independent variable.* The best way to remember this name is to recall that the variable is independent of the subject's behavior. As experimenters, we choose two or more levels of this circumstance to present, and nothing the subject does can change the levels of the independent variable. For example, if our independent variable is light intensity, then we might select high and low intensity as our two levels and observe our subject's behavior under both circumstances.

Dependent Variables

Once we have chosen the independent variable, we will want to measure a subject's behavior in response to manipulations of that variable. We call the behavior we choose to measure the *dependent variable* since it is dependent upon what the subject does. In the reaction-time experiment, for example, we want to find out whether there is a relationship between light intensity and time to respond. Thus, our dependent variable is the time from the onset of the light until depression of a button. It is sometimes useful to make a statement about the expected nature of the relationship. Such a statement is called a hypothesis. In the example, we might hypothesize that, the more intense the light, the quicker the response will be. The outcome of the experiment will determine whether the hypothesis is supported and becomes part of the scientific body of knowledge, or whether it is refuted.

Control Variables

So far, we have chosen one circumstance to manipulate (the independent variable). However, we will have other circumstances in an experiment that we will need to account for in some way. One possibility is to control them, thus making them into *control variables*. We can control such circumstances by seeing that they do not vary from a single level. For example, in our reaction-time experiment, we might require that the lighting conditions in the room be constant, that all subjects be right-handed, that the temperature be constant, and so on. Ideally, then, all circumstances other than the independent variable would stay constant throughout an experiment. We would then know that any change in the dependent variable must be due to the changes in the independent variable brought about by the experimenter.

There are several problems with the perfectly controlled experiment we have just designed. First, it is impossible to control all of the variables. Not only is it impossible to control genetic and environmental conditions, but it is impossible to force cooperative attitudes, attentional states, metabolic rates, and many other situational factors on our human subjects.

Second, we really do not wish to control all the variables in an experiment, for we put ourselves back in the box we were trying to extricate ourselves from; we create a unique set of circumstances. If we could control all variables while manipulating the independent variable, the relationship established by the experiment would hold in only one case—when all variables were set at exactly the levels established for control. In other words, we could not *generalize* the experimental result to any other situation. As a rule of thumb, then, the more highly controlled an experiment, the less generally applicable the results.

Suppose, for example, that General Nosedive from the Air Force came to you and said "Say, I understand you ran an experiment on reaction time. Tell me how intense I should make the fire-warning light in the F-111 so that my pilots will respond within half a second." Having conducted a well-controlled experiment, you reply "Sir, if you can guarantee that the pilot is a 19-year-old college sophomore with an IQ of 115, sitting in an air-conditioned, 10-foot-by-15-foot room, with no distracting sounds and nothing else to do, and if you always give a warning signal one second before the light comes on, then I might be able to give you an answer." You can probably imagine the general's reply. The moral of the story is—if you want to generalize the results of your experiment, do not control all of the variables.

Confounding Variables

Having established that we do not want to control all of the circumstances, what can we do with the remaining circumstances in our experiment? One possibility is to let them vary. However, since our goal is to make a clear-cut statement about the effect of the independent variable on the dependent variable, we must be careful that none of these other factors also vary with the independent variable. Any circumstance that changes systematically as the independent variable is manipulated is called a *confounding variable*.

Suppose, for example, that we used three light intensities in our reaction-time experiment: a low-intensity light for the first 20 trials, a medium-intensity light for the next 20, and a high-intensity light for the last 20. If we reported that "Subjects respond more quickly the more intense the light," someone else could say "No, subjects respond more quickly after practice." In fact, we could both be correct, or either one of us could be incorrect! The problem is that we have unintentionally *confounded* the experiment with a variable that changes systematically with the independent variable.

An experimenter can record the most sophisticated measurements, do the finest statistical test, and write up the results with the style of a Truman Capote, yet a confounding variable can make the whole effort worthless. A recent feud between Coca-Cola and Pepsi-Cola illustrates the type of confusion that can be caused in this manner.[1]* Pepsi pitted its cola against Coke in a drinkers' test in which subjects who said they were Coke drinkers drank Coke from a glass marked Q and Pepsi from a glass marked M. More than half of the subjects reportedly chose the glass containing Pepsi as their favorite. Coke officials countered by conducting their own preference test—not of colas but of letters. They claimed that more people chose glass M over glass Q not because they preferred the cola in glass M but because they liked the letter M better than they liked Q. This hypothesis was supported when most people tested still claimed to prefer the drink in the M glass when *both* glasses contained Coke.

In this example, the letters were apparently a confounding variable. Since they varied systematically with the colas in the original test, the drinkers' preference for the colas could not be distinguished from their preference for the letters.

Random Variables

We have decided to allow some circumstances to vary, and we have seen the importance of avoiding confounding variables. In what way can we allow the circumstances to vary and still be sure that they will not

---

* The superscript numbers refer to the references at the end of each chapter.

confound our experiment? One alternative is to permit some of the circumstances to vary randomly, these variables being termed *random variables*.

In using a random variable, we take a large number of measurements and assume that the general results of our measurements will resemble the real-life set of circumstances to which we wish to generalize. For example, if we want to generalize the results of an experiment to all students at a particular college, we should randomly choose subjects from that population. Or if we want to generalize our reaction-time results to a situation in which lights might occur in many locations, we should randomly select from among those locations.

There is no particular trick to random selection. Any device that allows each item in a population an equal chance for selection can be used. If there are two items in your population, you can flip a coin to select from it.* If there are six, you can throw a die. If there are 33, you can use 33 equal-sized slips of paper. Most mathematical handbooks and many statistics texts have random-number tables based on a process equivalent to drawing from 10,000 slips of paper. Using any column or columns in a table of random numbers, you can simply assign each of your items a number and select the item when that number occurs. If you happen to be a computer bug, you can use the computer to generate random numbers or events.†

If you have chosen to make a circumstance into a random variable, you must be sure that it varies in a truly random way, since not all events that appear random really are. Humans are notoriously bad at producing random events. For instance, if you try to randomize conditions in an experiment by assigning events yourself, you have not randomized! If you assume that subjects will show up for an experiment throughout the day or throughout the semester in a random order, you are wrong! People who are morning subjects or afternoon subjects or early-semester or late-semester subjects have different characteristics. Mistakes in randomization are commonly made by new experimenters. Don't you make them!

Randomization within Constraints

In some cases you may not wish to make a circumstance into either a random or a control variable. Actually, randomization and control define opposite ends of a continuum. Falling between these two extremes are various degrees of *randomization within constraints*. In this case, you control part of the event assignments and randomize the other part. Suppose in our reaction-time experiment we knew that practice could be an important variable. If we present all of the low-intensity trials first, followed by all of the high-intensity trials, then we could be accused of

---

*Actually, most coins are slightly biased in favor of heads, but, unless you are running an experiment with over 10,000 subjects, don't worry about it.

†Computers are also less than perfect at generating random events, but they're much better than coins. For the purpose of assigning events in an experiment, it doesn't make much difference which method you use.

confounding the experiment; any difference between response times to low- versus high-intensity light might, in fact, be due to short versus long practice. In order to avoid this problem, we could decide to control the practice variable and give only one trial to each subject. Or we could assign the low- and high-intensity trials randomly over, say, 12 trials by flipping a coin and presenting a high-intensity light whenever a head occurs and a low-intensity light whenever a tail occurs. This alternative might not be the most attractive, however, since it might result in an inadequate representation of high and low intensities. (The flipping of the coin might result in only three high-intensity trials, for example, and nine low-intensity trials.) In order to avoid this possibility, we decide to have an equal number of high- and low-intensity trials. Thus, as a solution we establish a constraint on the assignment of trials (an equal number of each type of trial), and we make a random assignment within this constraint. We might write the word *high* on six slips of paper and the word *low* on six and draw them out of a hat to determine the order of presentation. This procedure would fulfill the requirement that the conditions be randomly ordered across trials within the constraint that the two intensities be equally represented.

Other constraints, of course, are possible. We might wish to avoid the possibility that too many trials at a particular intensity occur early in the sequence. We could then *randomize within blocks,* with the block serving as our constraint. Using this alternative, we could choose three blocks of four trials each, assuring that two high-intensity trials and two low-intensity trials are randomly selected within each block. To describe this procedure, we would say that conditions were randomly assigned to three blocks of four trials each, with the constraint that each intensity be represented an equal number of times within each block.

Many such constraints can be legitimately used as long as they are specified. However, the more constraints you specify, the less random is your selection process and the less generalizable your results.

Figure 1-2 summarizes the general experimental model we have outlined so far. Since all circumstances in an experiment must be either controlled or randomized in order to avoid confounding the experiment, the circumstances on the left have been partitioned into an independent variable, control variables, random variables, and variables randomized within constraints. While partitioning the variables, we should keep in mind that a decision to control increases the precision of the results (because the circumstances are less variable) but decreases their generality. On the other end of the continuum, a decision to randomize decreases the precision but increases the generality.

CORRELATIONAL OBSERVATION

In establishing relationships that add to our knowledge of human behavior, it is not always possible to conduct an experiment. In such cases, a *correlational observation* is often appropriate. In a correlational observation we try to determine if two variables are related without attempting to experimentally manipulate either one. Suppose, for example, we

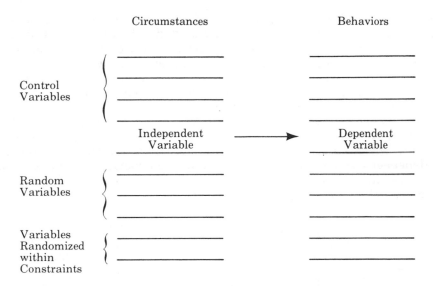

Figure 1–2. A diagram representing an experiment. One of the circumstances has been chosen as the independent variable. The others have been partitioned into control variables, random variables, or variables randomized within constraints. One of the behaviors has also been chosen as a dependent variable.

were interested in finding the relationship between parental discipline and rate of juvenile delinquency. To fit this problem into the experimental model, we would have to make parental discipline the independent variable and force the parents of a cross section of newborn infants to discipline their children at a particular level of strictness or leniency. When the children reach age 18, we might count the number of appearances before juvenile court for each child. Obviously, few parents would agree to such an experiment, nor would our society smile on our sincere effort to do good research. Rather than give up on what might be an important question, however, we could consider using a correlational observation.

In making such an observation, we could randomly choose a number of children and send their parents questionnaires asking such questions as "How often do you spank your child?" "Does your child have a specific time to be in bed?" and so on. Based on the answers to these questions, we could assign each set of parents a number on a scale from strict to lenient. We could then survey court records to determine the number of offenses for each child and determine if a relationship might exist.

Data* from correlational observations are typically pictured in a *scatterplot,* in which each variable is represented on an axis and each

---

*Every good experimenter must remember that *data* is a plural word; a datum is, but data are. If you chant to yourself "these data are" three times each morning when you wake up, you'll probably still forget!

point represents a single measurement. For example, hypothetical data from our parental-discipline study are plotted in Figure 1-3. In this case, each point represents the parental-discipline score and the number of court appearances for each child. This scatterplot shows that there is a moderate relationship between parental discipline and court appearances in our fictitious example. Children whose parents are strict tended to have fewer court appearances. Since we agreed at the beginning of this chapter that the business of scientists is establishing relationships between events, why is this result not as good as the result of an experiment? When we conduct a good experiment, we can conclude that the independent variable caused a change in the dependent variable. From a correlational observation, however, the best we can do is conclude that one variable *is related to* a second variable.

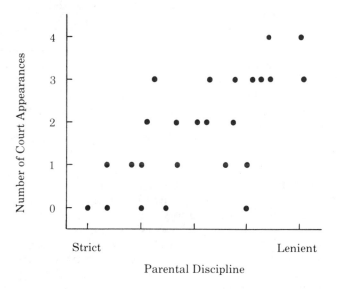

Figure 1–3. Fictitious data showing the relationship between parental discipline and the number of court appearances for children.

You may be wondering why we can't say that leniency *causes* juvenile delinquency in the same way that we can say that changes in an independent variable cause changes in the dependent variable in an experimental situation. Perhaps the following example will illustrate why it is difficult to make causal statements based on correlational observation. The Army conducted a study of motorcycle accidents, attempting to correlate the number of such accidents with other variables such as socioeconomic level and age. The best predictor was found to be the number of tattoos the rider had! It would be a ridiculous error to conclude that tattoos cause motorcycle accidents or, for that matter, that motorcycle accidents cause tattoos. Obviously, there is some third factor that is related to both—perhaps preference for risk. A person who is willing to take risks likes to be tattooed and also takes more chances on a motorcycle.

If we were to try to fit a correlational observation into our experimental model (Figure 1-2), we might say that the investigator has allowed all of the circumstances to become random or confounding variables. The experimenter has no control over any of the circumstances—including the circumstance of major interest. Rather than choose one of the circumstances as an independent variable and then manipulate that variable, the investigator would permit all variables to vary randomly and then sample from at least one variable. We cannot call it an independent variable, since the levels were not independently chosen by the investigator. For this reason, the chances are quite high that some other circumstance is changing along with the variable of major interest and causing the observed change in the behavior.

Another example of this problem is the Surgeon General's position on cigarette smoking and lung cancer. Although it had been known for some time that there was a positive correlation between the number of cigarettes smoked and the incidence of lung cancer, the Surgeon General was reluctant to say that smoking caused lung cancer. While some of this reluctance may have been politically motivated, much of it was justifiable scientific caution, for there could have been a third variable that caused the cancer but was related to smoking. For example, people who are nervous might produce a chemical that keeps the body in an irritated state, causing irritated cells that are prone to malignancy. It might also be true that nervous people smoke more cigarettes. Nervousness, then, could have caused the change in both variables.

Thus, the Surgeon General's office would have to perform an experiment in order to say definitively from one study that smoking causes lung cancer. Such an experiment might require 1000 people to smoke 40 cigarettes a day, another 1000 people to smoke 30 a day, and so on. In this design, experimenters could determine the probability that an individual in each group would have gotten lung cancer during his lifetime. Assuming that no confounding variables were present, any real difference in the incidence of cancer between the groups could be said to be caused by the cigarettes. Since the use of cigarettes would be independent of the subject's preference, the number of cigarettes smoked would be an independent variable. However, our society requires that a person's preference be honored, so ethically such an experiment could not be and was not conducted. How, then, did cigarette packs come to have the following warning printed on them: "The Surgeon General Has Determined That Cigarette Smoking Is Dangerous to Your Health"?

In this case, correlations were determined for many of the other variables that could have been related to cancer and smoking. As more and more of these variables were eliminated, it became increasingly likely that cigarette smoking was the cause. The Surgeon General apparently felt that all of the logically possible mediating variables had finally been eliminated. That fact, in combination with animal experiments that did show a causal relationship, convinced him that such a statement could be made.

In summary, then, we must sometimes collect correlational data to establish important psychological relationships. However, we must consider these data carefully to avoid the common error of interpreting the results of a correlational observation as a causal relationship.

NATURALISTIC OBSERVATION

There are some psychological questions that cannot be answered even with a correlational study. Some psychologists would argue that the act of filling out a questionnaire or reporting for an experiment could distort the behavior of a subject. Suppose we were interested in whether consumption of alcohol was related to social aggressiveness. We could set up an experiment in which groups of subjects drank measured amounts of alcohol. They would then interact while the experimenter sat in the room and noted the amount of aggressive activity. How aggressive do you think the drinkers would be in this situation? They would probably resemble a church congregation more than a bar crowd.

In order to get an effective answer to our question, we would probably have to go to a bar and observe its customers. This technique in psychological research is called *naturalistic observation* because experimenters observe behaviors under the conditions in which they normally occur. Naturalistic observations are required when we wish to investigate any behavior that we feel might be distorted by the artificiality of an experimental situation. Children, for instance, are typically inhibited by the presence of adults, particularly strangers. We would expect the behavior of children playing at home with their own toys to be far different from their behavior in a psychology lab with unfamiliar toys and a strange-looking psychologist present.

For a long time comparative psychologists* wondered whether any animal other than humans used tools, and naturalistic observation provided them with the beginnings of an answer. Initially, data collected by observing chimpanzees in zoos supported the general belief that other animals did not use tools. After a while, however, "chimpanzeeologists"

*A comparative psychologist is not someone who makes TV commercials in which Brand X loses out to Brand Y. A comparative psychologist compares the behavior of animals, including humans, across species. Comparative psychologists contend that the rest of us are far too egocentric in our research; humans form only a small part of the animal kingdom.

began to wonder if maybe zoo chimpanzees were not using tools because no tools were available in the zoo. They gave them tools like pliers and screwdrivers, but the chimps still didn't use them. Finally, a particularly bright investigator named Jane Goodall moved into the forest with the chimps. She lived with them and constantly observed their behavior for several years. One day she noticed that a particular chimp would take a wooden stick and dip it into a hole full of ants, then pull it out and lick off the ants that were clinging to the stick. Although it is not as sophisticated as a human's tools, investigators consider the stick an appropriate chimpanzee tool. Without naturalistic observation, chimpanzeeologists would still be sitting around watching zoo animals not using tools.

The problem with naturalistic observation as a research technique should be obvious to you after our discussion of confounding variables. Since the investigator has no control over any of the variables he or she is observing, it is possible that one variable may be changing systematically along with the primary one being observed. In our bar example, for instance, an investigator might observe that the more alcohol the customers drink, the more aggressive their social interactions become. However, the observer may not notice that as the evening wears on and more drinks are consumed, the number of bar patrons also increases. Maybe aggressiveness is related to crowding. Or perhaps the bartender is getting tired and brings the drinks at a slower rate. Maybe aggressiveness is related to frustration.

Thus, while naturalistic observation has an advantage in realism, it also has disadvantages in its lack of control. As with correlational observations, experimenters must be aware of potential confounding variables and must avoid making causal statements.

CASE HISTORY

The final research technique available to a psychologist is the *case history*. A case history is a detailed account of the relevant events in one person's life. Usually this account is purely verbal, with no quantification. If you were a therapist who had a pair of Siamese twins with dual personalities as patients, you might be interested in exploring why Siamese twins get dual personalities. You would immediately realize that trying to conduct an experiment to answer the question would be futile. Even if you could find enough Siamese twins around to do an experiment, it is considered unethical to make Siamese twins mentally ill; it is also unethical to make non-Siamese twins mentally ill!

You might next consider a correlational observation. Perhaps you could correlate the number of personalities in Siamese twins with degree of childhood stress. Again, you would need to find a number of Siamese twins who have dual personalities. Since this task is virtually impossible and a correlational observation based on one data point is meaningless,* you would also have to abandon this approach.

The only option left open would seem to be a case history outlining the factors in the lives of the Siamese twins that have contributed to their development. First you would spend many hours interviewing the twins in order to establish a history of their life from birth to present. In addition, you would talk with their relatives and friends and examine any school, medical, and psychological records that were available. Since all of this information would require far too much space to report, you would select what you felt were the most important aspects.

The case-history technique has built into it all of the dangers that have been mentioned for the other methods, including unknown confounding variables and inability to establish causality. This method also has additional pitfalls. For one thing, the investigator is generally trying to reconstruct past events from the subjective reports of those who were associated with those events, and research has shown that people are terrible at recalling the past. One investigator found that mothers were quite inaccurate about recalling the details of their pregnancy and the birth of their child six months to a year after the experience. You can imagine the problems involved when the memories are 20 years old!

A second possible pitfall of the case-history method is the investigator's bias in selecting events to be reported. In a psychology course, I was once required to support a particular personality theory using events from the life of the major character in the book *Crime and Punishment*. It was quite easy to select events that offered convincing support for my theory. However, I discovered that the other students in the class had used the same book to support three other personality theories, also in a very convincing way. They had either chosen different events or given a different interpretation to the same events I had chosen. Even with the limited set of events described in a single book, bias was extremely important in determining the relationships we established. Is it any wonder that an investigator can find support for his or her own pet theory from the nearly unlimited set of events in a person's life?

A number of books have come out recently that analyze the lives and personalities of famous historical figures, such as Richard Nixon, John Kennedy, and Sigmund Freud. Although they may make interesting speculative reading, they are subject to all of the dangers inherent in a case history. In addition, most of the events the authors use as support for their theories are based on second-hand reporting in the public media. Thus, they are one more step away from the objective truth. (For example, one author concluded that Nixon was psychotic, while another concluded that he was neurotic.)

---

*It is pretty hard to establish a relationship between two variables with a single point. It is not hard to establish a relationship with two points, however, since only one straight line can be drawn between them. Reporting a relationship based on two points is a lot like bragging—it's easy to do but no one pays any attention.

Thus, the case-history method obviously has many drawbacks. It should be used only when a person's life situation or behavior is so unusual that finding other similar cases would be virtually impossible. Interpretation of the events reported in a case history should always be regarded as speculative.

SUMMARY

As scientists of human behavior, psychologists have a number of research techniques available to them, all of which aim to establish relationships between events and to fit these relationships into an orderly body of knowledge. The experimental method, which is the primary focus of this book, requires that a particular circumstance called an *independent variable* be related to some aspect of behavior called a *dependent variable*. The other circumstances in a given experiment can be treated as *control variables, random variables,* or *variables randomized within constraints.* Throughout an experiment, investigators must guard against *confounding variables* that change systematically with the independent variable and distort the relationship between the independent and dependent variables. Sometimes when an experimental approach cannot be used, it is necessary to use *correlational observations* in which variables are observed and their relationship recorded. The results of such a study cannot be used to establish *causal relationships,* since none of the variables are under the control of the investigator. When the artificiality of the experimental approach would distort the results of an investigation, psychologists may use *naturalistic observation* as a method—that is, they observe behavior in a realistic setting. Finally, a *case-history* method may be necessary if an experiment is not appropriate and the potential number of observations is limited.

REFERENCES

1. Coke–Pepsi slugfest. *Time,* July 26, 1976, pp. 64–65.

How to Get an Experimental Idea 2

> A fair idea put to use is better than a good idea
> kept on the polishing wheel.*

> *As he was testing hypothesis number one by ex-*
> *perimental method a flood of other hypotheses*
> *would come to mind, and as he was testing these,*
> *some more came to mind, and as he was testing*
> *these, still more came to mind until it became*
> *painfully evident that as he continued testing*
> *hypotheses and eliminating them or confirming*
> *them their number did not decrease. It actually*
> *increased as he went along.†*

I was once so bold and foolish as to assign introductory psychology students the task of proposing seven experiments as a course requirement. At first I was puzzled by their reactions to this assignment. Above the din of gnashing teeth, the moaning, and the groaning could be heard the plaintive wail of my stupefied students, "How do we get an idea?" Not only did I find it difficult to understand why getting an idea would pose such a problem, I also found it impossible to answer the question. I have now pondered this pervasive problem and formed an opinion about why it occurs and what can be done to solve it.

I don't believe the problem is that students have no ideas. As small children, we are curious about everything, including human behavior: "Mommy, why is that man so fat?" "How does Jenny eat with her left hand?" "Why can't I spell as good as Betty?" "Why do Tommy's parents spank him so much?" I refuse to believe that this curiosity simply fades away. In fact, the same students who "could not get an idea" seem to have plenty of thoughts about human behavior at parties or bull sessions: "What's the best way to study for my bio exam?" "Should I marry him or just move in with him?" "Am I more creative in the morning?"

*Osborn, A. F. *The Journal of Creative Behavior*, 1970, 4, cover.
†Pirsig, R. M. *Zen and the art of motorcycle maintenance.* Copyright 1974 by William Morrow & Company, Inc. Reprinted by permission of the publishers, William Morrow & Company, Inc., and The Bodley Head.

FEARING EXPERIMENTAL IDEAS

For this reason I will refuse to believe you if you tell me you don't have any ideas for an experiment. It's not true that you don't have any ideas, but it may be true that you are afraid something is wrong with the ideas you do have! This fear can paralyze your natural creativity, and, after a while, all your ideas seem inadequate to you.

Such fears are usually irrational, stemming from a misunderstanding of psychology experiments. Psychologists call irrational fears *phobias.* Since I am a psychologist, I cannot resist the temptation to name the phobias behind our inability to get experimental ideas. The following phobias seem to be the most common.*

Geniephobia (Fear of Geniuses)

Geniephobia stems from the common belief that anyone doing research must be a genius and that your modest brainpower couldn't possibly measure up. Researchers often do little to counteract this belief, and a few have been known to cultivate it. For years, every time I read a

---

*Any resemblance of these names to accepted psychological terminology is purely coincidental.

journal article I pictured the author as a wise-looking old man with flowing white locks. It was quite a shock to find that many experimenters are actually young, ordinary-looking people who make silly mistakes and say stupid things just like the rest of us. My own geniephobia is still being cured. The more experimental psychologists I meet, the less I think only geniuses can do this kind of work.* So, relax. Your ideas are probably as good as theirs were when they were getting started.

A PREPHOBIC HAVING LOTS OF IDEAS

Imitatophobia (Fear of Imitating)

Those people with imitatophobia are afraid to propose any idea unless it is absolutely original. An imitatophobic who combines this fear with a belief that everything worthwhile has already been thought of often reaches a state of total paralysis. Truly original experiments are few indeed in psychology. Most experiments use variations of somebody else's method to test somebody else's theory. In the next chapter you will learn how to find out what other experiments have been done in your area of interest, and you will find out exactly how unoriginal you are. Don't be afraid to move science along in small steps, however. That's what the rest of us do.

Paraphernaliophobia (Fear of Apparatus)
and
Manuphobia (Fear of Doing It by Hand)

If the sum total of your mechanical knowledge of the automobile is that the right pedal makes it go and the left pedal makes it stop, you are a prime candidate for paraphernaliophobia. This malady will scare you

---

*I do not mean to imply that experimental psychologists are dumber than other scientists. Biologists and physicists can be dumb, too.

away from any experimental idea requiring apparatus more sophisticated than a deck of cards.

On the other hand, if you will not consider doing any experiment unless it requires sophisticated scientific equipment, you are a victim of the opposite affliction, manuphobia. Everyone knows that the more complex the equipment, the better the research.

Both positions are unfounded, however. Some of the best research uses little or no apparatus. Piaget developed a major area of child psychology with no more apparatus than toy blocks, water glasses, and modeling clay. Other areas of psychology, such as verbal learning, concept formation, attitude assessment, and personality, require no more than pencil and paper. Apparatus can help you do research, but it isn't the research itself. And when apparatus is necessary, there will be someone who can teach you how to use it.

Parsimoniophobia (Fear of Simplicity)

Parsimoniophobics think they must come up with grandiose experiments that will change the course of science in one fell swoop. Their motto is: If it's simple, it can't be science. While there are some advantages to complex experiments, generally you should aim for the simplest experiment that can answer your experimental question. People with parsimoniophobia seldom complete their majestic experiments; when they do, they usually cannot interpret the results. To start with, then, think simple. You can always pursue more complex questions later. (In Chapter 8 we will talk about what we mean by simple or complex experiments.)

Calculatophobia (Fear of Statistics)

Some people dread having to do any calculations tougher than counting their fingers. If you can never remember how to figure out your car's gas

A CALCULATOPHOBIC

mileage, or how to keep your checkbook straight, you are a potential calculatophobic. If you will consider only those experiments that require the simplest statistical tests, remember that such tests are tools that can help you interpret your results; they should not cause you to throw out good experimental ideas. You can always find someone who enjoys playing with numbers to help you analyze your data. I am not saying that a knowledge of statistics is unimportant, but it is, after all, just a tool used in science, not science itself.

Imperfectaphobia (Fear of Being Imperfect)

An imperfectaphobic will not tell you about an experimental idea until every tiny detail is perfectly worked out, and his or her proposal looks like the final report. This attitude often stems from having read too many pristinely presented journal articles. As we will discuss in Chapter 5, journal articles are end products; they seldom reflect the sloppy thinking and general air of confusion that precedes most experiments. Completed experiments are often quite different from the experimenters' original ideas. The original idea for an experiment simply forms the kernel; the experimental procedure itself will evolve as you set up and conduct the experiment. If you take the plunge and begin talking about your experiment in rough form, others may be able to help you mold it into a perfect experiment. Well, almost perfect.

Pseudononphonoscientiaphobia (Fear of Not Sounding Scientific)

People with this hideous affliction can only recognize a great idea if it is expressed in *scientific jargonese*.* Scientific jargonese is a pseudolanguage that some scientists make up to sound good when they talk with other scientists who do similar research. It helps obscure the research from the general public—and sometimes from other scientists as well. For example, in jargonese an experiment designed to determine if people remember words better when the words are in groups is described as an investigation into "the effect of taxonomic and categorical clustering on the retention of verbal material." Or a notion that people from ethnic groups live in the same neighborhood because of pressure from their friends is described as an experiment examining "the effect of demographic distribution by ethnic affiliation as a function of peer-group coercion." Jargonese can also be translated into everyday language. If you are interested in "the effect of affiliative preference on the salience of dimensions in person perception," you are actually trying to find out whether people who join certain organizations differ in the way they see

---

*I am using the word *jargonese* to represent the fourth dictionary definition of jargon (speech or writing characterized by pretentions, terminology, and involved syntax) as opposed to the first definition (the language peculiar to a particular trade, profession, or group). The line between jargon and jargonese is thin indeed.

other people. Try translating one yourself: "the effects of maternal employment on sibling aggressive tendencies."*

As you can guess from the way this book is written, I believe that most pseudoscientific jargonese is nonsense. Good scientists need not hide behind their language. A good idea is a good idea regardless of the words used to express it.

Ergophobia (Fear of Work)

Sorry, there is no known cure for this affliction.

Now that we are aware of what fears might block our creativity, let's try to get some experimental ideas. What is the best way to start?

OBSERVATION

Someone once said that it's easy to write: just sit at the typewriter and stare at the keyboard until drops of blood appear on your forehead. This also describes the best way to avoid coming up with experimental ideas. Since we are interested in human behavior rather than typewriter behavior, the best thing to do is observe humans, not typewriters!

Thus, getting experimental ideas is simply a matter of noticing what goes on around you. Once you become a good observer, your natural curiosity will provide you with experimentally testable questions. One week of constant observation should provide you with enough experiments to last three careers.

Indeed, some of the classic research in experimental psychology started with a simple observation. If Ekhard Hess' wife had not noticed that his pupils got bigger when he was looking at bird pictures, pupillometrics might never have gotten underway. If Ivan Pavlov had not noticed that his dogs were salivating to stimuli other than meat powder, Igor Nosnoranovitch might have been the father of classical conditioning instead. If Jean Piaget had not noticed that his daughter Jacqueline stopped making gurgling noises when she could no longer see her bottle, he might be a famous Swiss watchmaker today. Most revolutionary experimental ideas have been generated by simple observation.

Public Observation

After reading the next couple of paragraphs, take a paper and pencil, leave the room you are in, and walk outside where there are people to observe. As a training exercise in observation, make notes of possible experimental questions that occur to you as you stroll around.

---

* If you came close to "Do working mothers' kids fight more?" then you are catching on. Be sure to buy my next book: *Scientific Jargonese for Fun and Profit.*

First I'll go on a stroll to show you what I mean: I wander outside, and I see that the sun is shining.

1. Do people get more or less work done when the weather is nice?

I walk past two workmen laying concrete for a bikerack. One is working; the other is standing and watching.

2. Do workers stand around more when they are unionized?

A couple of joggers run by.

3. Do people who exercise regularly sleep better at night?

A young woman is sitting over there under a tree with a young bearded fellow. They are looking rather amorous, and I feel like a peeping Tom. Better move on.

4. Do women find men with beards more attractive than men without beards?

I see a large group of students filing into a classroom.

5. Do students in large lecture classes make better grades than those in small classes?

I arrive at a crosswalk. Will that car stop? Yes, it did. Across I go.

6. Are drivers more likely to give the right of way to pedestrians of the opposite sex?

I stop to watch a sport car zooming down the street.

7. Do people drive sport cars faster than regular cars?

I head back past the library.

8. Do students who study in the library retain information better than those who study in the dorm?

I pass the bikerack at the front of my office building and see lots of bikes.

9. Are ten-speed bikes easier to ride than three-speed bikes?

I lope upstairs to my office. I am back.
   I just got nine potential ideas for experiments. That's almost one per minute! Now you try it while I wait.

ME WAITING

Welcome back. Did you get plenty of ideas? Think of the ideas you could get if you were that observant all of the time. Now the problem is "which idea should I turn into an experiment?" because not all important questions can be answered by experiment. All experimental questions must pass the ROT test: they must be *Repeatable, Observable,* and *Testable.* For example, science cannot answer moral questions, such as: "Is abortion wrong?" "Is it proper for women to wear short skirts?" "Is dope evil?" While we can certainly use the scientific method to determine people's opinions about these questions, we cannot devise any test that could answer the questions themselves. We must therefore eliminate all such questions from any list of experimental ideas. Other questions fail because they are not observable: "Do dogs think like humans?" "Is my experience of the color red the same as yours?" Finally, some questions fail experimentally because they cannot be reliably repeated.

NOT ALL QUESTIONS
MAKE GOOD EXPERIMENTS.

Some supporters of ESP (extrasensory perception), for example, claim that it occurs only under certain conditions and that it is impossible to predict when the conditions are right. In other words, ESP works only some of the time. As long as this basic tenet governs ESP effects, it is impossible to test for the existence of ESP.

Do all of the questions in your list of ideas meet the ROT requirements? Take a moment to go through your list and eliminate any that fail to do so.

After reading Chapter 1, you should also recognize that some questions must be answered by correlational observation rather than by experimentation. For example, if as in question 7 we want to know whether people who choose to drive sport cars drive at a faster speed than those who drive other types of cars, then we must do a correlational observation to answer the question. On the other hand, if we wish to know whether any driver tends to drive faster when driving a sport car, we could design an experiment to answer the question. Take another look at your list of ideas, and label each idea experimental or correlational.

Our little walk has been interesting, but people in public provide us with a limited set of behaviors. Whom else can we observe?

Observing Yourself

As you may know, introspection was one of the earliest techniques in experimental psychology. Introspectionists, however, concentrated on looking at their own mental processes rather than their own behavior. Since a controversy developed about whether a person can know his or her own mental processes, experimental psychologists stopped watching themselves altogether. Rather than follow the dictum "Know thyself," they resolved to "Know not thyself."* It is still generally frowned on to do an experiment with yourself as the only subject; nevertheless, you can get some good experimental ideas this way. Not only will you be able to collect many samples of the behavior you are interested in, but you might even have some idea why you did what you did. The former can give you an idea for an experiment, the latter an idea for a theory.

With a little effort, you can begin to notice your own behavior. It may seem ridiculous to suggest that you do not notice yourself, but it is probably true. When dressing, which arm do you put into your shirt or blouse first? When you brush your teeth, do you brush the left side first or the right? Do you put the key to your house or room into the lock rightside up or upside down? When you cross your legs, do you put your left leg or your right leg on top more often? These are all things you do every day. Do you notice them? Observing yourself can be very entertaining† as well as a good source of ideas. Write down the ideas as they occur to you.

---

*Some experimental psychologists still don't know who they are.

†If you develop this skill, you will have to learn to control yourself in public. You may be considered quite strange if you break into gales of laughter over your own behavior.

KNOW THYSELF.

Observing Your Friends

Your friends are also good sources of experimental ideas. It is important, however, to observe their behavior in as unobtrusive a manner as possible. Staring is considered impolite at best and grounds for a fight at worst. People sometimes avoid paying attention to their own behavior because they are not particularly fond of it themselves. Consequently, to avoid losing friends, keep your observations to yourself. Pointing out your insights, no matter how brilliant, will not help you win friends and influence people.

Observing Children

Observing children is a necessity if you are interested in doing experiments in the area of developmental psychology, but children can also give you good ideas for other areas of research. If you are not blessed with* children, you probably have friends and relatives who would be more than happy to let you watch theirs for a while. Unlike adults, who have learned that their behavior should appear rational, logical, and consistent to an outside observer, children generally behave in ways that are uncomplicated by complex patterns or social inhibitions. Be-

---

* Or plagued by (depending on your point of view).

cause most kids couldn't care less about adult standards, you will be able to observe relatively uncontaminated behavior patterns in children.

Observing Pets

Animals are interesting to study in their own right, but much of their behavior can also be generalized to humans. Further, you will find that pets are even less inhibited than children; since they are less capable of highly complex behavior patterns, their behavior is often easier to interpret. In addition, you can manipulate your pet's environment without worrying quite as much about the moral implications of possible permanent damage (see Chapter 5 for a discussion of the ethics of animal treatment).

OBSERVE YOUR PETS.

VICARIOUS OBSERVATION

Although you may find it less exciting than direct observation, you can also get experimental ideas by reading other people's research. You might feel that this technique of *vicarious observation* feeds off other people's creativity, but nonetheless there are certain practical advantages to this approach. For one thing, because the broad experimental question you are researching already has a stamp of approval from the author and journal reviewers, you know that the questions being asked are considered important. Second, somebody else has already fit the experimental result into the existing body of knowledge, thereby structuring the area of research for you and saving you time and effort. Finally, earlier researchers have devised a method of attack that apparently works and that you may be able to modify and use in your research.

In beginning your search for an idea, you should first identify an area of research that interests you. You will then know what types of journals you should read. Your topic should be as specific as possible: competition in small groups, play therapy in schools, perception of visual illusions, development of arithmetic abilities, and so on. For the more general topics you specify, you can simply scan journals having related articles. For more specific topics, this procedure is rather inefficient, and you will need to do a literature search as described in Chapter 3. In either case, as you read the journal articles, make a note of the experimental questions left unanswered by the research. The author will sometimes help you discover what these questions are by suggesting where future research should go. You might select one of these experimental questions for your experiment.

EXPANDING ON YOUR OWN RESEARCH

Once you have done several experiments, you will find that your own research may provide many experimental ideas. Every experiment you do will leave a number of questions unanswered. For example, after using several levels of an independent variable in an experiment, you may want to see what happens when you choose other levels. Or you may have controlled a certain variable at a particular level in one experiment and wonder what would happen if you set it at a different level. Or you may come up with unexpected results and want to find out why the outcome was not as predicted. Each experiment usually brings up more unsolved questions than it answers.

This picture of science as a continual growth of new questions is quite different from that held by many people who conceive of science as a fixed body of knowledge we need only uncover. This latter concept views scientific research as leaving fewer and fewer questions unanswered as it proceeds. In reality, however, each experiment actually increases the number of questions to be answered. Instead of working ourselves out of business, we are working ourselves into more business than we can possibly handle.

This open-ended view of science can be very discouraging and very exciting. It can be discouraging because it is sometimes difficult to chart our progress through an ever-expanding universe in which we sometimes seem to take five steps backward for every step forward. On the other hand, it is exciting because we end up asking better and better questions. Perhaps the goal of science is not to find answers to all possible experimental questions, but to answer ever more promising and important questions. In following up on your own research, then, you will find that your main problem is not "How can I get an experimental idea?" but "Which idea is the most important one to work on?"

FOCUS ON A PRACTICAL PROBLEM

If you have a practical problem crying for a solution, you may also have the kernel of an experimental idea. So far in this chapter we have been pretending that all research is *basic research**—that is, research done

---

*Basic research is sometimes also called pure research, perhaps because one is not supposed to have mixed motives for doing it. Unfortunately, some of the people who do this kind of research seem to prefer other dictionary definitions of pure—for example, untainted with evil or guilt. I have never heard pure scientists defend the position that they are physically chaste, even though I suspect that this is the subconscious reason behind wearing white lab coats.

for the sole purpose of increasing the scientific body of knowledge. It is not necessary to justify such research as a solution to any practical problem, although basic research can help solve practical problems. Today's behavior-modification techniques, which provide some of the most powerful procedures for correcting human behavior problems, are based on basic research done in the rat laboratories of yesteryear. Adams[1] found that many of our military systems were designed using information from basic research done more than 20 years earlier. Thus, basic research does at times prove valuable for solving practical problems. In general, however, such research is done in the name of the advancement of science.

Research designed to solve a specific practical problem is called *applied research.* Perhaps you need to know how humans read handwritten numbers so that you can design a machine to automatically read ZIP codes. Or you may wish to know whether daily quizzes will improve a student's classroom performance on major examinations. Or you may want to know whether transactional analysis is a more effective therapy than psychoanalysis. Many such practical problems need immediate answers that basic researchers might never find. Needing an answer to a practical problem is a perfectly legitimate reason for doing research, and it can be very satisfying if your findings have an immediate impact on the world.

Observation is again the key to getting ideas for applied research. Finding a practical problem is simply a matter of carefully observing human behavior and permitting your curiosity free rein. As with the other procedures that we have discussed for getting experimental ideas, you will find that there are more practical problems needing to be solved than you can possibly do experiments to solve. As before, the question becomes, "What should I do first?" not "What can I do?" We will deal further with this question in Chapter 11.

SUMMARY

Although we all have natural curiosity about human behavior, many of us develop irrational fears that block our ideas. Some of us fear that all other researchers are geniuses and that our ideas will not be original. Some people are afraid to propose an experiment requiring complex apparatus, while others are afraid of experiments with simple apparatus. Others fear that their idea is too simple, that their experiment will require complicated statistics, or that their idea is not perfect when it is proposed. Finally, many people do not believe they have good ideas until they translate them into scientific jargonese.

The major key to getting experimental ideas is to learn to *observe* the world about you. You also need to know which ideas are scientifically appropriate. Ideas must be *repeatable, observable,* and *testable* to be experimental ideas. To get ideas you can observe yourself, your friends, children, and even your pets. Although the best ideas come from direct observation you can also get ideas by reading other people's research (vicarious observation) and from following up your own research. Finally, some of the best ideas come from having a practical problem that needs to be solved. Research designed to solve a practical problem is called *applied research,* while research aimed primarily at advancing scientific knowledge is called *basic* or *pure research.*

REFERENCES

1. Adams, J. A. Research and the future of engineering psychology. *American Psychologist,* 1972, *27,* 615–622.

How to Find Out 3
What's Been Done

Polonius: What do you read, my lord?
Hamlet: Words, words, words.*

Perhaps while you were reading Chapter 2, a terrific experimental idea came to you in a blinding flash of inspiration. On the other hand, an idea may have appeared with a dull thud. In any case, some interesting experimental idea has begun to form, and you may be getting eager to start your experiment. You should consider one thing first, however: your terrific idea may already have been somebody else's terrific idea.

WHY SEARCH THE LITERATURE?

Although psychology is a relatively young science, more than 4000 research articles are published in a typical year. While it is unlikely that another investigator has done exactly what you are planning to do, it is not unlikely that out of all the articles accumulated over the short history of psychology, somebody has done something quite similar. It would be counterproductive for you to repeat an experiment unless you, for some reason, did not think the results were reliable.

You might also find it helpful to discover how other investigators have attacked similar problems. Perhaps they have used experimental techniques with which you are unfamiliar. You might also find that other investigators have already discovered a number of pitfalls you would rather not waste your time rediscovering.

Science is an organized body of knowledge, not a random collection of facts built by scientists doing small isolated experiments. Thus, the most important reason for knowing what experiments others have done is that you will be required to fit your findings into this existing scientific body of knowledge. When you have completed your experiment, you will be required to say not only "This is how it came out" but also "This is where it fits in." In order to know where your work fits in, you obviously have to know what the body of knowledge was like prior to your

*Hamlet, Act II, scene ii, line 195.

experiment. This chapter discusses how to find out what is in that body of knowledge through a *literature search.**

While you are doing a literature search in the library, be sure to keep a record of what you find. Each time you find an article or book that might be useful, make a note of the important points and write down the complete reference. Include the names of the authors,† the title of the work, the name of the journal or book, the date, volume number, page numbers, and for a book, the publisher. You will need all of this information later if you decide to refer to the article in your experimental report. Some people find it helpful to use an index card for each reference. The more orderly you are the first time through, the less time you will waste later looking for references that you put on the back of a long-lost gum wrapper.

---

* Psychologists traditionally have called this process a literature search despite the sneers of Shakespeare and Dickens buffs who probably would not call journal articles "literature."

† People who are new to psychology sometimes find it strange that experimental psychologists talk about experiments by author rather than by subject. If you hear your instructors say such things as "The Carothers, Finch, and Finch, 1972, findings agree with Peterson, Bergman, and Brill, 1971," they are talking not about law firms but about experimenters.

THE TIMELINESS OF SOURCES

Assuming you have found your way to the library as the most logical place to conduct your search, where do you start once you are there? One good way to learn about the sources available and how up-to-date each source is is to follow the history of a typical experiment as it is communicated to the scientific community. Figure 3-1 summarizes this process on a time line in which zero represents the time a project is started. After the investigator collects his data, he may present preliminary results to a small gathering of friends at his local institution. Assuming he isn't laughed out of the room, he may decide to attend a professional meeting such as an annual convention and read a paper summarizing his research.* Again, assuming that this somewhat more hostile audience gives him a little support, he might decide to write a manuscript based on the research and submit it to a journal. If the article is accepted, it will appear in the journal about nine months to a year later. Following journal publication, *Psychological Abstracts* will publish an abstract of the article. If it is an important article, it might appear later in the *Annual Review*, be cited in other articles, and perhaps be mentioned in a publication such as *Psychological Bulletin*. Finally, after many years, a textbook author might mention the research as part of the accepted body of knowledge.

Figure 3-1 points out the *time lag* involved in the scientific communication process. If you use the library, your first access to an experimental result is its appearance as a journal article. As you can see, you will have lost considerable time at this point since the research was probably started at least three years before its publication in a journal. If you then immediately begin your experiment and go through the same process, the other author will have to wait three more years before your results will be reported in a journal article. (Even the U.S. mail has better turn-around time than this!) Because of the need to avoid such delays, fewer than one in seven research efforts originate from formal sources such as journal articles.[1] Most ideas originate from more informal communication among scientists in a given field. However, as a new investigator without the contacts necessary for such informal communication, you might have to be content with the formal sources for the time being. If you continue to work in a particular area of research for a while, you will find out who else works in your area and will get to know your fellow researchers personally. You will then be ahead of the journals and the new new investigators.

In the following section we will consider each of the formal sources in more detail, discuss the advantages and disadvantages of each, and determine how to locate relevant sources. Let's start with books and work our way to more recent sources.

---

*This is where your professors go when they miss class. And you thought they were on vacation having fun.

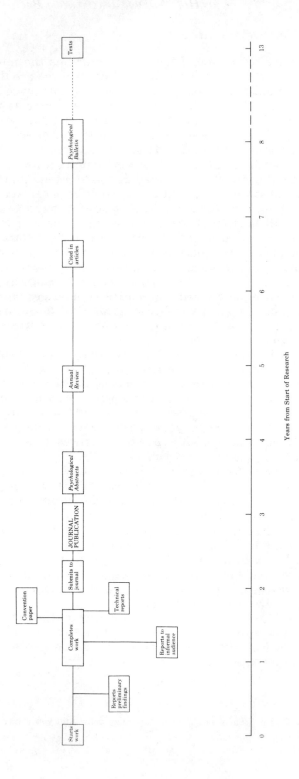

Figure 3-1. The publication history of research from its inception until its appearance in the psychological literature. (Adapted from "Scientific Communication: Its Role in the Conduct of Research and Creation of Knowledge," by W. D. Garvey and B. C. Griffith, *American Psychologist,* 1971, 26, 349–362. Copyright 1971 by the American Psychological Association. Reprinted by permission.)

FORMAL SOURCES

Books

Since books only include research that was begun an average of 13 years earlier, you might think that books would be the worst possible source. However, this enormous time lag makes them the best source as well as the worst source. A very important process occurs between the time research is completed and the time it is reported in one of the sources: the research is screened on the basis of importance and quality so that by the time it appears in a book it has been integrated with other research to form a coherent body of knowledge. Thus, the value of book research lies in the fact that the author thinks it is well done and important and that it fits into the growing body of knowledge. The author has already done much of your work for you; it's just a bit obsolete.

A good place to start your literature search, then, is to find a recently published book that deals with the general research topic you are interested in. If the author has done a good job, you can have some confidence that you have a good summation of the most important research from the start of psychology up to about 13 years prior to the publication date of the text. Your job is now considerably easier: to find out what has happened during the last 13 or so years.

One problem with this approach is that the author has had to be selective and has not been able to include all of the research done on a particular topic since the beginning of psychology. Each book author is biased toward some theoretical approach or methodological approach and selects research based on this bias. Thus, to be sure you can trust the author's scholarship and bias, try to develop a consensus of several resource books; at the very least, try to discover the author's particular bias.

There are several ways to find appropriate books. The library card catalog is, of course, a primary source. If you can identify your research area by related topics in the card-catalog index, you will have no problem identifying appropriate books.* Prior to your library visit, you might also look in an introductory psychology book under the topic you are interested in. Most basic texts will reference some suggested readings that can start you out. Finally, you might talk to an instructor in your psychology department who does research in the area. He or she will probably be happy to give you some book references.

Review Articles and Books

Several other sources make an attempt to summarize and integrate research within particular areas of psychology. These sources are more up-to-date than textbooks, and consequently there has been less time for the research to be put into perspective. One such source is a journal

---

*Although, as my consulting editor points out, actually finding the books in many libraries can be more difficult.

published by the American Psychological Association called *Psychological Bulletin.* The inside cover of this publication states that "The *Psychological Bulletin* publishes evaluative reviews of the research literature in psychology. It includes reviews and interpretations of substantive and methodological issues." Here are some sample titles from recent issues of the *Bulletin:*

> Cross-Cultural Research in the Perception of Pictorial Materials
> Organizational, Work and Personal Factors in Employee Turnover and Absenteeism
> Sleep-Assisted Instruction
> Effects of Inferotemporal Lesions on the Behavior of Monkeys
> Spontaneous Remission in Adult Neurotic Disorders: A Revision and Summary
> Initial Drug Abuse: A Review of Predisposing Social Psychological Factors
> Outcome Studies in Mental Hospitals: A Review
> Modality Effects in Short-Term Verbal Memory

As you can see, the topics covered in these articles are generally narrower than textbook topics. A *Bulletin* article may also take a previous summary article as its starting point rather than the beginning of psychology and fall short of a complete survey. Nevertheless, a recent review article can save you a great deal of search time. And now you are only about eight years behind.

For those experiments that are quite similar to the one you are planning, a review article will not go into enough detail for you. In this case, the original sources cited at the back of the article will allow you to quickly find which references are important and to determine how your experiment will fit in with past research.

Another source of research reviews is the *Annual Review of Psychology,* published by Annual Reviews, Inc. This series of books is published one volume per year, with the topics varying from year to year depending upon the decision of an editorial board. Each chapter is written by an author who is a recognized expert in the field he or she is writing about and whose job is to bring the field up-to-date by summarizing and integrating the research done since the topic was previously included in the series. The topics are generally broader than *Psychological Bulletin* topics:

> Personality
> Developmental Psychology
> Spatial Vision

However, some topics are a bit narrower:*

> Intervention Techniques: Small Groups
> Social and Cultural Influences on Psychopathology

---

* Did you notice the interesting relationship? The broader the topic, the shorter the title.

Finding out whether the *Annual Review of Psychology* has covered your area recently should take you less than a minute per volume, since only a few topics are covered in each volume. Surveying *Psychological Bulletin* articles, however, will take somewhat longer. Fortunately, a journal called *Psychological Abstracts* can save you some time because it lists all psychological literature. Various monographs and reports from annual conferences also review and summarize research; you will find them in *Psychological Abstracts* as well, listed along with regular journal articles. (We will discuss how to use *Psychological Abstracts* shortly.)

Journal Articles

Psychological journals form the backbone of our science. They are called *primary sources* because they present the basic results as interpreted by the experimenter or experimenters who did the research rather than by third parties such as those who compile reviews. To do a really thorough literature search, you must use journal articles. As you recall, they are the most up-to-date of the formal sources, following the actual research by about three years. Thus, whereas article authors try to integrate their work with the existing body of knowledge, their effort can be only partly successful since they cannot know about other research being done at the same time. Therefore, you will have to do some integration yourself in order to make the research form an orderly body of knowledge.

We cannot possibly list all the journals related to psychology here. Many professional organizations publish journals for their members, with a number of publishing companies sponsoring individual journals as well. However, to give you an idea of the kinds of journals available, here is a listing of the journals published by only one organization, the American Psychological Association:

American Psychologist
Contemporary Psychology
Developmental Psychology
Journal of Abnormal Psychology
Journal of Applied Psychology
Journal of Comparative and Physiological Psychology
Journal of Consulting and Clinical Psychology
Journal of Counseling Psychology
Journal of Educational Psychology
Journal of Experimental Psychology: General
Journal of Experimental Psychology: Human Learning and Memory
Journal of Experimental Psychology: Human Perception and Performance
Journal of Experimental Psychology: Animal Behavior Processes
Journal of Personality and Social Psychology
Professional Psychology
Psychological Bulletin
Psychological Review

Psychological Abstracts

As you can see, it would be nearly impossible to look through every article published in every journal since psychology began. Fortunately, there are publications that have done this survey for you. *Psychological Abstracts,* for example, will be your main tool in doing a literature review. Published monthly by the American Psychological Association, *Psychological Abstracts* publishes an abstract or short summary of every article published in the field of psychology in all countries of the world. It also abstracts books, review articles, and government documents. The *Abstracts* scans a total of about 100 journals and reports regularly and further simplifies your task by classifying and indexing each abstract by topic and author.

Using the *Abstracts* can seem a bit frightening at first. Some students who know about *Psychological Abstracts* still do not use it because they are not familiar with a few simple procedures that make it easy to use. When you locate it in your library, you will find a complete wall of rather imposing books staring at you. Glancing in one of the books, you will find paragraph upon paragraph of terse-sounding summaries and lists of authors and terms. Once you understand how to use the journal, however, you will find that it is only slightly more difficult than using a dictionary.

LITERATURE SEARCH

Let's begin by discussing what happens to an article when it is processed by *Psychological Abstracts.* Several months after an article is published in a journal, an abstractor will put together one of the listings you see in the journal. The listing will be given a number. The authors will be listed, followed by parentheses containing the first author's institution. Next comes the title of the article, the name of the journal the article appeared in, the date of appearance, the journal's volume number, and the page numbers for that article. If the author wrote a summary of the article, this abstract will follow. If not, the abstractor will write one and include it. Here is a typical but fictitious listing:

> 4603. Follicle, Harry R. (Southern Idaho State U.) Beard growth during sexual fantasy. *Journal of Whisker Behavior,* 1977 (Jun), Vol 3 (4), 444–447. —Exposed one group of Papago Indian males to appropriate stimuli for sexual fantasizing while isolating a second group. The weight of the hair shaved from the face of each subject was measured daily to see whether sexual fantasizing is related to beard growth. It was concluded that Papago Indians do not have sexual fantasies since none of the subjects produced measurable facial-hair growth.—Journal abstract.

To help you find the listing, the abstractor adds the name of each author and the listing number to an author index at the end of each monthly issue. In addition, the abstractor determines several key words that describe the article and includes these in the subject index. Suppose the article is about the effects of *cannabis resin* (a marijuana-type drug) on the social behavior of mice. The key words "cannabis" and "animal social behavior" would be added to the subject index along with the number for the listing. Finally, the abstractor would determine the major classification and subsection classification for the listing. In the previous example, for instance, the major classification would be "Psychopharmacology" and its subsection would be "Physiological Intervention and Drug Effects." The abstract would then be grouped with other articles on the same topic in the monthly issue.

Psychological Abstracts publishes a semiannual index for every half-year of abstracts. Some libraries will also have cumulative indexes that cover a period of two or three years. Let's pick a topic and see how you would use a semiannual subject index to search a half-year period of time. Suppose you want to know whether being the oldest child in a family affects a person's success in school. If you looked under the subject of "Birth Order" in the *Jan.-June 1975 Subject Index,* you would find 17 listings, such as:

> birth order & academic behavior in continuing education course, severely disadvantaged adults, 6180.

Because this article seems relevant to your subject, you would make a note of the listing number. Others that you might want to examine more closely would be:

> birth order & social class, college attendance, 8340.

> self-image & self-esteem & academic achievement & birth order & needs & legalization attitudes, female college student marihuana users vs. non-users, 9647.

Some of the listings would not be worth your time, such as:

> firstborn's role in family & community relations, African tribal & oriental cultures, 2910.

Once you have jotted down the numbers of all likely looking articles, you can look up the original abstracts from the previous half-year's *Psychological Abstracts,* deciding as you go whether each reference is worth looking at more closely. If you are still interested after reading the abstract, write down the reference, find it in the library, and read the complete article. At each point of your search, you need look at only enough information to determine whether to pursue each reference. In this manner you can search through large amounts of material very efficiently.

If you have never used *Psychological Abstracts* you might find it helpful to select several specific topics, head for the library, and try your hand at finding relevant articles. If you cannot think of any topics,* try these:

> The attitude of various races toward segregation
> Differences in emotional adjustment of smokers and nonsmokers
> Leadership capabilities of female managers
> Brain-hemisphere effects on motor skills
> The effect of alcohol on traffic accidents

Once you have used the subject indexes to find all of the research related to a particular topic you might wish to double-check by using the author indexes. Look up the names of the authors of the articles you have tracked down to make sure you have identified all of their relevant work. Find the listing numbers of any additional articles and again select relevant articles based on their abstracts.

The *Psychological Abstracts* will give you access to all of the formal sources except those articles less than about six months old. To be thorough, look at the article titles from the final half-year of the journals in which you have previously found relevant research.

"Treeing" through the References

There is another way to do a literature search that is not nearly so thorough as using *Psychological Abstracts.* However, it is a good way to determine whether you have missed any key research in your previous search. I will refer to this technique as *treeing backward through the references.* The first thing to do is find the most recent article that deals with the topic of interest; this article will form the "trunk" of your research tree. Find the references at the end of the article. Quite a few of these references should also be relevant to your topic (hopefully most

---

*If you cannot think of any topics, you must have missed Chapter 2. Go back and read it!

of them are already on your list). Each of these articles will also have a reference list from which you can select in the same way. Follow each reference list backward through the literature until you have found all of the important articles that form a new set of branches on your tree. This method can be quite helpful, but do not rely on it as your sole technique, since you cannot always assume that every author has done a scholarly job of finding the important references.

TREEING THROUGH THE REFERENCES

You can also tree forward through the references once you have found a key article that is several years old. However, for fear of boggling your mind with too much information at this point, I am putting this discussion in Appendix A at the end of the book. Appendix A also includes information on government publications called technical reports and on how to have an automated literature search done for you.

While a literature search is not particularly difficult to do, it can be very time-consuming* and not particularly inspirational since it involves lots of paper shuffling. Knowing the literature, however, is an

---

* One of the most time-consuming and exasperating things that can happen is to uncover references that have been ripped off or ripped out. It's enough to make the most ardent pacifist have fantasies of catching the scalawags and hanging them by their thieving thumbs in the town square.

absolute necessity. Nothing is more embarrassing when presenting the results of your life's work than to hear someone remark "You are, of course, familiar with Klip and Klap, 1976, who did this same experiment last year?"

INFORMAL SOURCES

Professional Meetings

As we mentioned earlier, to be completely up-to-date on the research in a particular field, you must become familiar with informal sources of communication. About 15 to 18 months prior to journal publication many investigators present their research at a professional meeting by reading a paper. In fact, about one-fifth of the articles published in major psychology journals are based on material previously presented at an American Psychological Association (APA) convention.[1] The APA annually sponsors a national meeting and six regional conventions. In addition there are many other non-APA professional meetings, such as those of the Psychonomic Society, the Psychometric Society, the Human Factors Society, and so on.

Of course, you can't attend every single meeting or convention in your field. Thus, some of the meetings publish papers in a bound volume called a proceedings, which is available in most libraries. In addition, shortly after the APA meetings, a journal called the *American Psychologist* publishes convention programs listing the author and title of each paper presented. You might also find that some of the faculty in your psychology department are members of these organizations and get programs prior to the meetings. Once you know that one of these papers is of interest to you, simply send the author a reprint request. You will understand the paper better if you read it than if you listen to it anyway.

The real reason for attending conventions, aside from engaging in superfluous hedonistic activities,* is to talk to other researchers presently doing work in your area of interest. Depending on how defensive they are, you might even find out what they are planning to do in the near future. In this way, you can fill in the information gap between "initiates work" and "convention presentation" in Figure 3-1.

By the way, if you learn something in one of these discussions that you might wish to quote in an article, be sure to write it down, note the date, and get the person's permission to use it. You can then cite the source in an article as a *personal communication*.

After you have established these informal contacts, you can work out an agreement by which other investigators routinely send you *preprints* of articles and papers as soon as they are finished. You, in turn, agree to send them preprints of your work. Sometimes a number of researchers working in a specific area will join to form a preprint

* Havin' fun!

group.* Usually, however, informal contacts are more valuable when they are on a one-to-one basis.

While the written record of our science is maintained by the formal sources, the informal sources also perform a vital service for science. They offer a forum for saying stupid but creative things. Your informal colleagues will chuckle quietly and tell you where you are wrong. Your formal colleagues are forced to guffaw loudly and boisterously tell the world where you have gone wrong. With only the formal sources, few of us would have the courage to try to move science by leaps and bounds, and we would stick with small conservative steps. The encouragement and friendly discouragement offered by informal contacts are important in shaping our thoughts into a form suitable for the formal literature.

I have tried to make this discussion of searching the literature as complete as possible. I hope that in doing so I haven't made the process sound more complex than it really is. Many new investigators believe that a literature search requires some sort of mystical powers and many years of experience. However, if you follow the simple steps outlined in this chapter, you will find that doing a thorough literature search can be a straightforward, satisfying experience.

SUMMARY

A *literature search* is necessary to find out if your experimental idea has already been investigated, to determine whether similar experiments

---

*I was once a member of a collection of psychologists interested in human decision making that was quaintly called "the group." Unfortunately, as "the group" grew, some groupers turned into groupies and rules had to be made. The group also became larger and more ritualized. Suddenly we were an institution! At that point informal lines of communication became formal, the purpose was lost, and the group faded away.

have been done, and to see how your experiment will fit into the current body of knowledge. In order to do this search efficiently, you should understand the lines of communication within the scientific community and the *time lag* associated with various sources of information. It is usually most efficient to begin your search in *books* that are relevant to your area of interest. Books describe research from the beginning of psychology up to about 13 years prior to current research. You can then use *review articles* to bring you within five to eight years of current research. *Journal articles* will form the backbone of your literature search. You can track down relevant articles through the subject indexes and author indexes from *Psychological Abstracts*. You can then double-check your search by *treeing backward through the references* of recent journal articles. Informal sources such as *papers read at professional meetings, personal communications,* and *preprints* are a valuable way to learn about current and future research.

REFERENCES

1. Garvey, W. D., & Griffith, B. C. Scientific communication: Its role in the conduct of research and creation of knowledge. *American Psychologist*, 1971, *26*, 349–362.

How to Be Fair with Subjects 4

> Whatsoever ye would that men should do to you, do ye even so unto them.*

> Our data show that the social structure of competition and reward is one of the sources of permissive behavior in experimentation with human subjects; the relatively unsuccessful scientist, striving for recognition, was most likely to be permissive. . . .†

You may think that we have now done all our preliminary work and are ready to start planning an experiment. First, however, we should consider one more issue—the ethics of doing a psychology experiment. As experimenters, we can be unethical in at least two ways. We can mistreat the people (or animals) whose behavior we are measuring. We can also mistreat the body of knowledge that we are trying to establish—in other words, treat our science unfairly. This chapter will discuss treating our subjects fairly; Chapter 5 will discuss treating science fairly.

Society as a whole and the scientific community in particular have agreed on a set of rules by which we must do our research. Some of these rules are unwritten, such as the basic rules of courtesy. The assumption is that such rules are so obvious that everybody understands them. Other rules are written, such as the *Ethical Standards of Psychologists*[1] and the *Ethical Principles in the Conduct of Research with Human Participants*,[2] both published by the American Psychological Association. These rules are continually revised as society's conception of the role of experimentation and the rights of an individual change. In this chapter we will first consider the relationship between the person doing the experimenting and the one being experimented on, including some basic courtesies in the relationship. Then we will discuss how this relationship can affect the outcome of an experiment. Finally, we will discuss alternative experimenter-subject relationships.

---

*Matthew 7:12.
† Barber, B. The ethics of experimentation with human subjects. *Scientific American,* 1976, *234,* 25–31.

TREATING HUMAN SUBJECTS FAIRLY

Since our purpose in doing an experiment in psychology is to understand human behavior, we will usually be interacting with humans. Traditionally, psychologists have referred to the people who will provide the behavior as *subjects*. The early forefathers and foremothers of psychology probably liked this term because it sounded scientific. Unfortunately, the term implies that people will be subject to the experimenter's will, or even worse, subjected to it! Back in the 1930s it was suggested that the term *experimentee* should be used in place of *subject*, but the suggestion never caught on.[3]

This discussion may seem pretty trivial to you—what's in a word? In this case, the word *subject* reflects the nature of the experimental relationship and as such suggests certain ethical considerations. Subjects are represented as passively reacting to the conditions of an experiment much like chemicals passively react when combined in the laboratory.

In the early history of experimental psychology, nobody worried about what to call the people who were experimented on since the experimenter and the subject were the same person. In those days, psychologists reported their own internal experiences as the dependent variable in their experiments. Since experimenters felt that only time and training made it possible to become aware of these internal experiences, they considered themselves their own best subjects.

Later in the history of psychology, many experimenters came to feel that verbal reports of internal events were inappropriate data for the science of psychology. Arguing that it is not possible to be objective and subjective at the same time, these experimenters started a revolution in psychology. Some psychologists, overreacting to the revolution, decided that only animal subjects were appropriate for psychology experiments. If you do not want a subject to make verbal reports, pick one who cannot talk! During this era, the rat became a prime subject for experimentation. Other investigators felt that while experimenters are too experienced to be experimented on, rats are rather unlike most humans. What was needed was a naive human. The naive human chosen was the college student. Today from 70% to 85% of published research[4,5] and as much as 90% of research conducted by university psychology departments[6] uses college students as subjects.

In this latest view, the subject is supposed to be a naive, well-motivated observer who will react to experimental manipulations in an uncontaminated way. Yet, as we shall see, subjects are not uncontaminated observers. They usually have definite ideas about the experiment they are serving in, and they attempt to achieve specific goals that are often different from the experimenter's.

Humans (even college students) also have certain legal and moral rights. A physicist can take the block of wood from his inclined-plane experiment and drop it, hammer on it, swear at it, kiss it, or do any number of things with it. Although his colleagues may think he is pretty weird, they would not have him arrested or throw him out of the profession. Psychologists, however, must preserve their subjects' rights at all times.

The nature of the experimenter-subject relationship makes our subjects particularly vulnerable because the experimenter usually has most of the power. For example, many subjects serve in experiments in order to satisfy part of a psychology class requirement. Under these circumstances, students may feel that their course grade will be affected if they fail to do as the experimenter asks. On the other hand, if subjects are paid for their services, they may feel that noncooperative behavior will earn them less money. Finally, if subjects volunteer for experiments because they believe they can advance the science of psychology, they may feel that society will benefit most from their cooperation. In any of these cases, subjects see the experimenter as having the ultimate power to evaluate or manipulate their behavior.

98-POUND
SUBJECT

SUPER
EXPERIMENTER

In addition to these academic, monetary, or altruistic motives for cooperating with the experimenter, subjects may also share the commonly held opinion that psychologists have a mysterious bag of tricks for determining whether someone is cooperating. The first three sentences between a psychologist and a stranger illustrate this belief: "What do you do for a living?" "I'm a psychologist." "Oh, are you analyzing me?" For some reason, many people believe that psychologists have X-ray vision and can look deep into their minds and find out what they are thinking. They believe they had better cooperate or the experimenter will get 'em! This belief, although it is sheer nonsense, again helps stack the experimenter-subject relationship in favor of the experimenter.

Rules of Courtesy

To unstack the relationship a little, experimental psychologists need to follow a code of behavior that treats their subjects with respect and

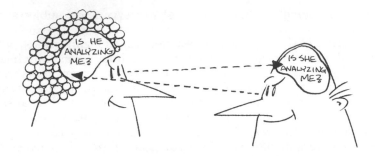

dignity. As a new experimenter, you should hang a sign in your experimental room (an imaginary sign is OK) that says "Subjects are humans too!" Subjects deserve the same courtesies you would give anyone who offered to help you with a project. Some simple rules of courtesy you should follow are:

1. *Be present.* Too often experimenters forget that they had a subject signed up or fail to notify the subject if the equipment broke down or if the experiment is delayed or called off for some other reason. Once a subject signs up for an experiment, you should make every effort to fulfill your obligation to be present for the experiment.

2. *Be prompt.* A subject's time is valuable too. Don't waste it.

3. *Be prepared.* You should rehearse all phases of the experiment prior to meeting any subject. Not only is it discourteous to do otherwise, but if you stammer over the instructions, tinker with the equipment, and generally fumble and mumble your way through the experiment, subjects may become so confused or disgusted that they perform poorly.

4. *Be polite.* Unless the experiment calls for it, ask your subjects to do something, don't order them. Make liberal use of the words "please," "thank you," and "you're welcome."

5. *Be private.* Treat all information that a subject gives you within an experimental context as confidential. Be discreet not only about what the subject tells you but also about how he or she performs on the experimental task. Federally funded grants are now quite specific about what information you may obtain from a subject, how you may use that information, and how to code and store it. If possible, eliminate subjects' names from data sheets, and use a method that will prevent others from discovering the identity of individual subjects.

6. *Be professional.* It is not necessary that you be so sober and stiff that your subjects feel uncomfortable, but do not be so casual and flippant that you convince your subjects that you do not care much about the experiment. They won't care either! Nor is an experiment the proper place to make dates, hustle golf partners, sell insurance, or use the experimenter-subject relationship for any purpose other than research.

While these rules seem simple enough, not all ethical issues concerning human subjects are so straightforward. More controversial issues, such as "What constitutes informed consent?" and "Should mental stress be permitted?" are discussed at length in *Ethical Principles in the Conduct of Research with Human Participants* mentioned earlier. However, no publication can cover all possible ethical issues, so most research-oriented institutions now have human-experimentation committees made up of established researchers and sometimes physicians and other technical experts. These committees screen all research proposals using human subjects. All federally funded and most institutionally funded human research must pass such a committee before it can be done.

Such review committees certainly help eliminate or revise many potentially unethical investigations. However, screening committees in the biomedical field have themselves recently been the subject of research, for it has been found that a significant minority of the people who serve on such committees are very poor at balancing the risks and benefits of human research.[7] A large majority of committee members surveyed had received no formal training of any kind in research ethics. So while these committees can be helpful, the primary responsibility for doing ethical research still lies with you, the experimenter.

The nature of the experimenter-subject relationship is important not only in terms of the subject's rights but also in terms of the experimental outcome. Although experimental psychologists like to pretend that subjects in psychology experiments are neutral creatures reacting in a sterile controlled environment, most know that such is not the case. In the next section we will consider in more detail how the experimental situation can influence the outcome of an experiment.

Demand Characteristics

When subjects show up for an experiment, they have very little idea what they will be required to do, but they are usually very interested in the experiment and want to know exactly what it is about. Experimenters in turn are often quite secretive about their intention, which prompts the subjects to try to determine what the experiment is really about from clues the experimenter gives them. The experiment then becomes a problem-solving game for the subjects.

These clues that influence subjects in the experimental situation have been called *demand characteristics* because they demand certain responses from subjects.[8] Whereas the experimenter provides many such clues, subjects also bring demand characteristics with them to the experiment. Based on having taken a psychology course, having read about psychology experiments, or even having been told about your experiment by a friend, subjects may bring such expectations as the following with them: The experimenter is going to shock me. The experimenter is trying to find out how intelligent I am. The experimenter is going to trick me into revealing something nasty about myself.

Sometimes these notions are so overpowering that a subject cannot be swayed from them. I once had a subject who was required to memorize a set of words presented to him through earphones. Shortly after starting the experiment, he tore off the headset and shouted "This thing is shocking me!" Thinking he might be right, I carefully measured for any current passing through the headset. The headset was well-grounded. I tried to continue the experiment, but the subject still claimed that he was being shocked. He had made up his mind that I was going to shock him and would not believe otherwise. As a result, his data had to be discarded.

Other demand characteristics come from subtle cues that the subject picks up during the experiment. To minimize such cues, experimenters attempt to standardize all experimental procedures. An experimenter usually reads instructions to subjects from a written copy, for example, so that all subjects at least will have the same verbal demand characteristics. In some experiments, however, even the way the experimenter reads the instructions can affect the subject's performance. In one experiment, two sets of tape-recorded instructions were made by experimenters who were biased toward opposite experimental outcomes.[9] The experimenters found significant differences between the performances of subjects hearing different tapes. Although the experimenters read the same instructions, the subtle differences in their voices apparently produced results consistent with their biases.

Even animal subjects seem to be influenced by subtle cues given by the experimenter. In one of the more famous experiments on experimenter bias, student experimenters trained rats to run a maze.[10] Some of the experimenters were told that their rats had been specially bred to be bright, fast learners; the others were told that their rats were bred to be dull, slow learners. The supposedly bright rats learned to run the maze in fewer trials, even though they were in fact littermates of the supposedly dull rats. The usual reason given for this result is that the student experimenters must have treated the rats differently, playing with the "bright" rats more and handling them so that they became less fearful of being manipulated. However, other investigators have claimed that the results might be due to student experimenters cheating with their data.[11] Whatever the reason, the experimenter's bias was reflected in the outcome of the experiment.

Cooperative subjects. After human subjects determine in their own minds what the demand characteristics of the experiment are, they will react according to their attitude toward the experiment.[12] Most subjects tend to be *cooperative* and try to fulfill the perceived demands of the experimenter. Some subjects cooperate to an astounding degree. In one experiment testing cooperativeness, the experimenter gave the subject a stack of 2000 sheets of paper and asked him to compute the 224 addition problems on each page. Although this task was obviously impossible, the subject continued to add for five and one-half hours, at which point the experimenter gave up! In a second experiment, the experimenter instructed subjects to tear up each sheet into at least 32 pieces after completing the additions. Again subjects persisted in the task for several hours without appearing hostile.

In order to see how this desire to cooperate might be behind a subject's response to demand characteristics, consider the following experiment on group pressure: A subject is brought into a room with six other people. The subjects are asked to judge which of two lines is longer. The first few problems are easy and everybody agrees. Then two lines are presented, and our subject is sure that the top line is longer, but everybody else says the bottom line is longer. After a long pause, the subject finally agrees that the bottom line is longer. What happened in this experiment?

The experimenter designed the experiment to find out whether group pressure can cause someone to make an obviously incorrect response. The other "subjects" in the room were confederates or stooges trained by the experimenter to lie on the appropriate trial. Since the real subject gave in to the group pressure, the experimenter feels that his hypothesis has been confirmed. But let's read the mind of our subject* and see what really happened: "Well, here's another pair of lines. The top line is definitely longer. What a dumb experiment this is! Why waste our time having us do such an obviously easy task? And why are we doing it as a group? The experimenter must be trying to see if we can influence each other. Sure enough, everybody else is saying the bottom line is longer. They couldn't possibly really think that. Let's see, I could either give in to these shills and agree or hold my ground. I want to be a good subject so I can get out of here. Besides, I'm sure that a group of people can get someone to change his mind, so I might as well agree. Besides, the experimenter seems like a nice guy and I don't want to mess up his experiment."

If our mind reading is correct, then our experimenter was wrong in his conclusion. The subject, who is only trying to be cooperative, can cooperate us into drawing an incorrect conclusion!

---

* See, psychologists *do* have mystical powers.

Defensive subjects.   Some subjects are less concerned with making the experimenter look good than with making themselves look good; let's call them *defensive subjects.* Such subjects search for demand characteristics in the same way that cooperative subjects do, but they use them differently. Usually a subject trying to perform as well as possible is an asset to an experiment. However, in some experiments, particularly attitude-assessment experiments, these subjects can cause problems.

Suppose we are investigating the difference in the way Chicanos and Anglos view sex-role behavior in children. We post one sign-up sheet requesting volunteers who have Spanish surnames and speak Spanish as a first language and a second sheet requesting Anglos who meet neither of these criteria. Now we show each subject pictures of children in traditional sex roles (such as girls playing with dolls) and in nontraditional sex roles (such as boys playing with dolls). We then ask the subjects to rate the acceptability of each behavior. Suppose more Chicanos than Anglos report that they find the nontraditional behaviors acceptable. We might conclude that Chicanos are more liberal than Anglos. On the other hand, another interpretation is possible. The members of each group of subjects were aware that they were selected on the basis of ethnic origin. Suppose the Chicanos were more concerned with upholding the pride of their ethnic group than were the Anglos. In this case, they may have bent over backward to keep from looking like socially unacceptable chauvinists. In other words, they appropriately perceived the demand characteristics of the experiment and attempted to defend their ethnic group.

In an actual experiment that demonstrated the defensive subject's reaction to demand characteristics, experimenters asked subjects to tap a key with their right and then their left index finger.[13] Tapping rates are usually faster for the preferred finger, but one group of subjects was told that graduate students at Yale and Michigan had been found to tap the key at similar rates with each finger. A second group was not given this information. The difference between tapping rates for the two fingers was significantly smaller for the first group. Again the subjects perceived the not-so-subtle demand characteristics of the experiment and tried to make themselves look as good as possible.

Noncooperative subjects.   Some subjects are neither cooperative nor defensive but downright *noncooperative!* The result of such behavior has been picturesquely called the "screw-you effect."[14] The noncooperative subject attempts to determine the demand characteristics of an experiment and then behave in such a way as to contradict the experimenter's hypothesis. Such subjects act out of any number of motives. They may be participating to fulfill a course requirement and resent being coerced. Or they may be opposed to the whole idea of studying human behavior scientifically. Or perhaps they are simply turned off by the experimenter. Whatever the reason, such subjects can be a real nuisance in an experiment. One way to eliminate noncooperative subjects is to set some minimal standard of performance so that you may exclude any subject's data that fall below this standard. This standard should be determined prior to the experiment and noted when the experiment is reported. Even this procedure will not eliminate the data of all noncooperative subjects, however. Sometimes the best we can do is attempt to give the subjects a positive impression of our experiment and hope that they will be cooperative.

How to Minimize Demand Characteristics

Although we cannot completely eliminate demand characteristics from an experiment, we should make every attempt to minimize those demand characteristics that might become confounding variables. It is important to know whether a change in a subject's behavior is due to the experimenter's manipulation of the independent variable or to the subject's perceived demand characteristics. There are several ways to minimize confounding caused by demand characteristics.

Automation. Demand characteristics can be controlled by *automating* as much of the experiment as possible. We have already discussed the use of tape-recorded instructions as one type of automation. Experimenters are often rather poor at reading instructions anyway, particularly after reading them aloud 20 or 120 times. You can also ask a person who is unaware of the expected outcome of the experiment to record the instructions if you want to minimize experimenter bias caused by voice inflections.

I have also used videotaped instructions in some of my own experiments. Videotape is particularly effective because it combines visual and aural modes during instruction. If experimental trials involve complicated sequences of events, sample trials can be presented at a slow enough rate for subjects to follow, thereby eliminating the need for the experimenter to go back and explain earlier portions of the instructions.

In some of today's laboratories, computers are used to play all or part of the experimenter's role in an experiment. Some investigators program the computer so that a subject never sees a human experimenter: The subject shows up at the appointed time. A sign instructs him or her to be seated at the computer terminal and press a button. The computer then presents the instructions by teletype or cathode-ray tube. The subject indicates his or her understanding of the instructions, and the experiment proceeds. The general idea behind this approach is that if we cannot assume that subjects are the passive automatons we once thought they were, then we can turn experimenters into automatons instead. However, some researchers object to this procedure on the grounds that the artificiality of the situation not only causes the subject to feel dehumanized but also decreases the generalizability of the results. This procedure also requires that subjects be able to read and understand the instructions, which makes it unsuitable for some subjects: children, rats, and college sophomores?

Blind and double blind. A second way of minimizing demand characteristics transmitted by the experimenter is to make the experimenter *blind* to the level of the independent variable being presented.

For example, I once did an experiment to determine if it was possible to "feel" colors with the fingers. Subjects were blindfolded and given three cards, two red and one blue. On each trial they were required to put the two cards that were alike in one stack and the one that was different in another. I was concerned that I might unintentionally signal subjects when they were correct by changing my breathing rate, coughing, or grunting when they had the cards correctly arranged. Some of my ESP-believing friends even suggested that I might send subjects ESP messages when they were correct! To avoid such signaling, I sat behind a screen so that I could not observe the subjects. I was thus "blind" to the color they were feeling. In fact, this procedure is sometimes called *double blind* since neither the subject nor the experimenter is aware of the experimental levels.

Unfortunately, experimenters cannot always be blind to the manipulation of the independent variable. For example, an experimenter who wants to measure the response time to either a single light or one of four lights and who has no way of automating the experiment will obviously know which condition is being presented. Nonetheless, for those experiments most likely to be affected by experimenter bias, you should make every effort to use a blind procedure.

Multiple experimenters. A third way to deal with experimenter-caused demand characteristics is to use *multiple experimenters*. In this case you will not control the experimenter variable, but you will let it vary by using random assignment of the available experimenters. Such a procedure will increase the generality of your result and decrease the chances that a single, blatantly biased experimenter will influence the outcome.

*Are Demand Characteristics
a Problem in Your Experiment?*

Even when you have attempted to minimize demand characteristics, they can creep into your experiment. Here are some procedures for detecting them:

Postexperiment questioning.   For a number of years following the revolution against subjective verbal reports, experimenters seldom questioned subjects about their impressions of an experiment. Fortunately, today many experimenters routinely seek this information from their subjects following the experiment. Such information can be valuable not only for uncovering demand characteristics but also as a way of forming new hypotheses that can later be tested in a formal experiment.

Postexperiment questioning can take many forms, from the experimenter asking an offhand question to a well-structured written questionnaire. If you want to be sure you uncover demand characteristics, you should plan your questions ahead of time.

In planning your questions, make sure that the questions themselves do not have demand characteristics built into them. For example, in the group-pressure experiment we discussed earlier, a biased question would be "You weren't aware that the other subjects weren't real subjects, were you?" The question itself demands that the subject say "no." If subjects say "yes," they thereby admit that they were not the naive cooperative subjects they agreed to be. They also put themselves in the position of telling the experimenter that the experiment was a waste of time because their data cannot be used.

You should also plan your questions so that they go from general, open-ended questions to specific, probing questions. For example, in one experiment designed to determine whether humans could be conditioned without being aware of it, subjects were asked to talk about any topic they wished and to continue until asked to stop.[15] Whenever subjects said a plural noun, the experimenter nodded, said "good" or "uh huh," and was generally reinforcing. As subjects continued to talk, they used plural nouns more and more frequently. As evidence that the subjects were unaware of the conditioning, the experimenters asked the postexperiment question "Did you notice that the experimenter was doing anything peculiar as you talked?" The subjects reported that they had not. Other investigators, not convinced by this experiment, did a similar experiment but followed the original question with progressively more specific questions, such as "Did you notice that the experimenter would respond when you said certain words?" Although the subjects had trouble verbalizing it, most of them were aware that "the experimenter was happier when I talked about certain things, like listing parts to cars." Further, the subjects who mentioned this awareness were the same ones who had shown the effect of conditioning. Thus, in order to determine whether subjects are influenced by demand characteristics, we should ask questions related to specific demand characteristics as well as asking more general questions.

Nonexperiments. Another way to determine whether demand characteristics could have affected the experimental outcome is to compare a *nonexperiment* control group with an experimental group.[12] The nonexperiment control group is not exposed to manipulation of the independent variable at all. They are simply told about the experiment, given the instructions, shown any apparatus, and then asked to describe how they think they would perform if put into that situation. If their prediction is quite similar to the outcome of the experimental group, then they were able to detect demand characteristics; these characteristics, rather than the independent variable, could have caused the outcome of the experiment. If their prediction is quite different from the experimental outcome, then demand characteristics probably did not cause the observed behavior.

Simulation control groups. You might also have subjects *simulate* their performance by pretending they have been exposed to a certain level of the independent variable and then showing you how they believe they would react. For example, in a hypnotism experiment you might ask members of a simulation control group to pretend they are hypnotized. If their behavior is indistinguishable from that of the real subjects who are hypnotized, then it is possible that the performance of the hypnotized subjects is due to nothing more than suggestibility and demand characteristics.

Alternative Experimenter-Subject Relationships

In the beginning of this chapter was the naive subject. And the naive subject was pleasing in the sight of the experimenter. But not all naive subjects are good; most are not even naive. So far we have been considering ways of keeping the subject as naive as possible, or at least discovering when the subject cannot be considered naive. We have another alternative, however. We can give in to the fact that subjects are not naive and make use of their problem-solving ability.

Deception and role-playing. One way to use this problem-solving ability is to give subjects false cues so that their interpretation of the demand characteristics is incorrect. This procedure of *deception* is a very controversial topic in psychology on both moral and methodological grounds.

The moral argument for deceiving subjects goes something like this: Although we may temporarily mislead subjects, we are justified because we are contributing to the advancement of science. Certain experiments must depend on a certain amount of deception. For example, how can we find out whether a bystander will come to the aid of someone in trouble unless we deceive the bystander into believing that the person is really in trouble? Eliminating deception in psychology experiments would mean eliminating all of social psychology and most of personality research. Besides, we always tell the subjects the truth at the end of the experiment.

The moral argument against deception goes something like this: You can use a term like "misleading" if you wish, but that is just a nice way of saying "lying." There is enough dishonesty in the world today without being dishonest in the name of science. How many of these "scientifically justifiable" experiments have caused great leaps forward in science? Not many! We can devise alternative ways of doing many of the experiments anyway, such as having subjects role-play. It is naive to think that debriefing subjects at the end of the experiment wipes out all effects of the deception. At the very least, such an experience will make them wary of anything they are told in future experiments and perhaps lead them to distrust all psychologists. The costs of deception are just not worth it.

The latter role-playing argument is testable. Some experimenters have tried to use both deception and role-playing under the same conditions and then compare the results. In *role-playing* the experimenter asks subjects to imagine that they are in a particular situation and to respond as they think they would in a similar real-world situation. If you were interested in bargaining behavior, for example, you might ask one subject to imagine that he is a labor leader, another subject to pretend that she is the president of a company, and a third to act like an arbitrator. You then operate under the assumption that their responses will in some way resemble those of people in the same real-world situation.

Unfortunately, while there are experiments that do report equivalent results from deception and role-playing,[16] there are many others that do not.[17] It is also difficult to specify the conditions under which similar results can be expected from the two methods. In many respects role-playing experiments are very much like the simulation control mentioned in the previous section. Perhaps role-playing simply reflects the demand characteristics of the experiment, rather than allowing us to predict what behavior would occur in a real-world situation.

We are still left with the original problem: when is deception justified, if ever? The American Psychological Association has published a statement that may help us answer this question:

> Openness and honesty are essential characteristics of the relationship between investigator and research participant. When the methodological requirements of a study necessitate concealment or deception, the investigator is required to ensure the participant's understanding of the reasons for this action and to restore the quality of the relationship with the investigator.*

The APA also suggests the following guidelines for deciding whether to use deception:

*From *Ethical Principles in the Conduct of Research with Human Participants,* by the American Psychological Association. Copyright 1973 by the American Psychological Association. This and all other quotations from this source are reprinted by permission.

1. The research problem is of great importance.
2. It may be demonstrated that the research objectives cannot be realized without deception.
3. There is sufficient reason for the concealment or misrepresentation that, on being fully informed later on, the research participant may be expected to find it reasonable, and to suffer no loss of confidence in the integrity of the investigator or of others involved.
4. The research participant is allowed to withdraw from the study at any time, and is free to withdraw the data when the concealment or misrepresentation is revealed.
5. The investigator takes full responsibility for detecting and removing stressful aftereffects.

If you follow these guidelines and ask for the advice of other investigators, you will probably avoid seriously abusing your subject's rights because of deception. We have by no means resolved the issue, but such discussion may help you rationally balance the costs and benefits of deception.

Naturalistic observation. We have already mentioned this final alternative to the standard experimenter-subject relationship in Chapter 1. *Naturalistic observation* depends on the experimenter's being an unobtrusive observer. Rather than having subjects pretend to be in a bargaining role, for example, the experimenter might go to an actual bargaining situation and observe behavior. We have already discussed the problems associated with this method. Experimenters usually have little control over the variables in the situation. They often have to wait for them to occur naturally, and even then they cannot control potential confounding variables or draw causal conclusions from the correlational data.

In this section, we have discussed the problems of treating subjects as naive uncontaminated observers. At the very least, therefore, we should be aware of the problem-solving nature of subjects and design our experiments so that the effects of subjects' problem-solving attempts can be evaluated. Where possible, these attempts should work for us rather than against us. Remember, subjects are humans too. Remember?

TREATING ANIMAL SUBJECTS FAIRLY

Some experimental psychologists use animal subjects in their research and have other ethical issues to consider. It is popular to make fun of the "rat runner" as an irrelevant eccentric. However, contrary to the belief that some experimenters use rats as subjects because they get along better with rats than with humans or because they get their kicks by torturing rats, there are valid reasons for using animals in some types of research.

Simpler Behaviors

If we view human behavior from an evolutionary perspective, then we can hypothesize that some of the most basic human behavior patterns are also present in the lower animals since certain behavioral abilities occurred early in evolutionary history. Thus, animal research is based on the assumption that we can investigate certain universal *basic behaviors* using lower-order animals. We know that, over time, the animals up the evolutionary line kept basic behaviors but also acquired more complex behaviors that tended to override the basic behavior patterns. Thus, if we are interested in studying basic behaviors, it may be not only possible but preferable to use animals that display the basic behaviors unconfounded by the more sophisticated patterns of behavior shown by higher-order animals. However, we must be careful when we attempt to generalize the behavior of an animal to humans. Human beings are obviously much more complex than rats, and no reputable investigator suggests that rat behavior is the same as human behavior. Although some less reputable interpreters of animal research have been known to overgeneralize findings out of ignorance or simplemindedness, such occasional misuses of animal data do not invalidate the original premise behind using animals.

Control

In addition to theoretical reasons for using animals in research, there are a number of practical reasons. For one thing, animals are available nearly all of the time. For some reason college students insist on taking weekends and holidays off. Animals can also be used for experiments that take place over a long period of time.* It is also possible and legal to *control* the conditions under which animals exist, both in and out of the experiment. Thus, animal experimenters can investigate such interesting variables as overcrowding, sensory deprivation, wake-sleep cycles, and environmental stressors.

With animals we can control their heredity as well as their environment—a task made easier by the fast reproduction and multiple births common to lower animals. In human research, heredity is seldom a controlled variable. In animal research, it is often a controlled or constrained variable. It is not true that "anything goes" with animals, however. We will discuss animal ethics shortly.

Uniqueness

Some animals also have *unique characteristics* that make them more appropriate for certain types of research. For example, fruit flies not only reproduce very quickly but also have large simple chromosomes. Squid have much larger nerve cells than humans and so lend themselves to investigation of nervous-system structure. Similarly, many animals have a larger portion of the central nervous system devoted to the sense of smell or the sense of balance than we do. In such cases, humans are simply not the best subjects for research.

---

*Although sometimes the inconsiderate buggers die on you. Rats!

Permanent Damage

Finally, lower animals are often used when the research could be *permanently damaging* to the structure or function of the animal. Ablation research can be done only with animals since it requires that a portion of the nervous system be purposely destroyed in order to observe behavioral consequences. Likewise, humans cannot be used in experiments requiring that electrodes be sunk into the central nervous system. In many cases this type of research also requires that the animal be destroyed and a histology* performed to locate the specific structural changes.

Manipulations such as keeping animals socially isolated can also cause permanent damage. One famous example of this procedure was the work in which infant chimps were separated from their mothers shortly after birth and then presented with various artificial mothers to determine what the important mothering dimensions were.[18] People frown on using human babies for such research.

Once we have decided to use animals as research subjects, what are the rules that govern our fairness toward animals? A general guideline for experimental animals is to make their lives as pleasant as possible and, when necessary, their deaths as quick and painless as possible. The caricature of the experimental psychologist as a ghoulish vivisectionist who derives pleasure from torturing animals is, of course, completely false. Most investigators actually grow quite fond of their animals and treat them as well as possible simply because they like them. Most mistreatment probably stems from ignorance about correct handling procedures. If you plan on using animal subjects, you should familiarize yourself with a number of publications. A booklet entitled *Guide for*

---

* Histology usually involves examining the tissue of the nervous system to see what has been destroyed or where the electrodes were placed. The brain is stained and sliced into very thin pieces for microscopic examination.

Laboratory Animal Facilities and Care can be obtained from the U.S. Government Printing Office, Washington, D.C., 20402. In addition, most states have now published laws stating minimum requirements for maintenance and handling of animal subjects for medical and behavioral research. Certain species require specific handling procedures to avoid diseases and behavioral problems, so you might also find it helpful to visit other laboratories that use the particular species you are interested in. Often these laboratories are able to give advice that will save you time and money and save your animals unnecessary hardship.

At times psychological experiments, by their very nature, subject an animal to stress and pain. In such situations, you should be convinced that the potential scientific gains are worth the costs before starting your research, and you should be able to defend your decision. Many institutions now have committees composed of qualified peers and experts to screen animal research as well as human research. However, you should consider these committees as imposing only minimum standards. You must satisfy what should be a more stringent standard of ethics—your own.

SUMMARY

This chapter discusses the ethical and methodological issues of treating human and animal subjects fairly. Since most of the power in the experimenter-subject relationship lies with the experimenter, it is important that the experimenter follow certain basic rules of courtesy. The experimenter must be present, prompt, prepared, polite, private, and professional. Although we have assumed in the past that human subjects are naive observers in the experiment, they are in reality problem solvers who are sensitive to the *demand characteristics,* or hidden cues, of the experimental situation. How subjects react to these demand characteristics depends on whether they are *cooperative, defensive,* or *noncooperative* in the experiment. We can minimize the demand characteristics by *automating* much of the experiment, by using a *blind* or *double-blind* design so that the experimenter is unaware of the specific conditions the subjects are responding to, or by using *multiple experimenters.* If unwanted demand characteristics are present in an experiment, we can sometimes detect them through *postexperiment questioning* of the subject or by using *nonexperiment* or *simulation* control groups. An alternative to assuming that subjects are naive is to use their problem-solving natures and give them false demand characteristics in order to deceive them about the actual purpose of the experiment. Alternatives to deception are to ask subjects to *role-play* or to observe them in a *naturalistic* setting.

Psychologists also use animal subjects in experiments because they exhibit some of the same basic behavior patterns that humans do in a form unconfounded by more complex behaviors. They also provide an opportunity for greater environmental and genetic control, as well as possessing certain unique characteristics that make them superior for certain types of research. While it is sometimes necessary for animal subjects to suffer *permanent damage* from an experimental procedure, we should adopt a code of ethics that allows us to make their lives as pleasant as possible and their deaths as quick and painless as possible.

REFERENCES

1. American Psychological Association. *Ethical standards of psychologists.* Washington, D.C.: Author, 1972.
2. American Psychological Association. *Ethical principles in the conduct of research with human participants.* Washington, D.C.: Author, 1973.
3. Rosenzweig, S. E. G. Boring and the Zeitgeist: Eruditione gesta beavit. *Journal of Psychology,* 1970, 75, 59–71.
4. Smart, R. Subject selection bias in psychological research. *Canadian Psychologist,* 1966, 7, 115–121.
5. Schultz, D. P. The human subject in psychological research. *Psychological Bulletin,* 1969, 72, 214–228.
6. Jung, J. Current practices and problems in use of college students for psychological research. *Canadian Psychologist,* 1969, *10,* 280–290.
7. Barber, B. The ethics of experimentation with human subjects. *Scientific American,* 1976, *234,* 25–31.

8. Orne, M. T. On the social psychology of the psychological experiment: With particular reference to demand characteristics and their implications. *American Psychologist*, 1962, *17*, 776–783.
9. Adair, J. G., & Epstein, J. Verbal cues in the mediation of experimenter bias. *Psychological Reports*, 1968, *22*, 1045–1053.
10. Rosenthal, R., & Fode, K. L. The effect of experimenter bias on the performance of the albino rat. *Behavioral Science*, 1973, *8*, 183–189.
11. Barber, T. X., & Silver, J. J. Fact, fiction, and the experimenter bias effect. *Psychological Bulletin Monograph Supplement*, 1968, *70*, 1–29.
12. Adair, J. G. *The human subject*. Boston: Little, Brown, 1973. See Chapter 2 for a complete discussion of subject attitudes.
13. Rosenberg, M. J. The conditions and consequences of evaluation apprehension. In R. Rosenthal & R. L. Rosnow (Eds.), *Artifact in behavioral research*. New York: Academic Press, 1969.
14. Masling, J. Role-related behavior of the subject and psychologist and its effects upon psychological data. In D. Levine (Ed.), *Nebraska symposium on motivation*. Lincoln: University of Nebraska Press, 1966.
15. Krasner, L. Studies of the conditioning of verbal behavior. *Psychological Bulletin*, 1958, *55*, 148–170.
16. Greenberg, M. S. Role playing: An alternative to deception? *Journal of Personality and Social Psychology*, 1967, *7*, 152–157.
17. Orne, M. T. Hypnosis, motivation and the ecological validity of the psychological experiment. In W. J. Arnold & M. M. Page (Eds.), *Nebraska symposium on motivation*. Lincoln: University of Nebraska Press, 1970.
18. Harlow, H. F. The nature of love. *American Psychologist*, 1958, *13*, 673–685.

How to Be Fair with Science 5

Science is willingness to accept facts even when they are opposed to wishes.*

To obtain a certain result, one must wish to obtain such a particular result: if you want a particular result you will obtain it.—Lysenko†

In this chapter we will continue our discussion of ethics, but here we will think about treating science fairly. In some respects, science has fewer defenses than a subject does. Animal subjects scream and yell and sometimes die when mistreated. Human subjects scream and yell and sometimes sue when mistreated. Science can't even scream and yell. If you mistreat it long enough, however, your fellow scientists might eventually scream and yell.

You might wonder how you can be unfair to an inanimate thing like science. In one sense, science *can* be considered animate in that it is a moving, changing, and hopefully expanding body of knowledge. New research constantly replaces or builds upon old findings and theories. Anything you do that retards the expansion of science or causes it to expand in the wrong direction can be considered scientifically unethical.

Science has a few safeguards built into it to ensure that the body of knowledge will continue to expand in a proper direction. For example, before you are allowed to report the outcome of an experiment in the scientific literature, a group of scientists who have been selected for their research accomplishments will review it. This review establishes whether the research appears to follow the rules of experimentation discussed in this book. Further, the reviewers attempt to determine whether your contribution is sufficient to warrant using the limited number of pages available in the journals. In this way the reviewers and editors of our journals attempt to screen research so that only competent

* Skinner, B. F. *Science and human behavior.* New York: Free Press, 1953.
† Lerner, I. M. *Heredity, evolution, and society.* San Francisco: Freeman, 1968.

and relevant findings are added to the body of knowledge.* While this reviewing process is not perfect, most psychologists feel that it accomplishes this important screening function rather well.

While the review system is designed to exclude research that was poorly done or that fails to make a large enough contribution, it was not designed to determine whether an investigator who may be capable of doing good research has lied about his or her research. People who know the rules and say that they have followed them when in fact they have not cheat science. Such behavior is usually geared toward making personal gains of some sort: "They weren't going to promote me unless I had five publications"; or "I had to make our product look good"; or "I had to have a positive result on the experiment to get a passing grade."

For the purposes of this discussion, I will define cheating as reporting that something happened in an experiment when, in fact, it did not happen or, conversely, failing to report something that did happen. My use of the term *cheating,* then, does not necessarily imply that the behavior is unacceptable, since, by this definition, some forms of cheating are considered acceptable. The general criterion we will establish for determining whether an action is acceptable will be: does the action lead to an efficient expansion of our scientific body of knowledge? If the answer is "no," then the action is unacceptable.

We can further subdivide unacceptable cheating into moderate cheating and blatant cheating. While the distinction is not always clear-cut, moderate cheating is any behavior that leads to verbal reprimands by fellow scientists, whereas blatant cheating is any behavior so harmful to the body of knowledge or to the scientific process that a person's privileges as a scientist are taken away.

BLATANT CHEATING

Dry-Labbing

One form of blatant cheating is to *dry-lab†* an experiment—a term coined by chemists to describe experimenters who never wet a test tube. Such "experimenters" know that the easiest way to run an experiment is not to run it at all. They do not have to bother with such mundane matters as buying equipment, signing up subjects, or learning to do statistics. All they have to do is learn to write up experiments (dry-labbers better read Chapter 9). Dry-labbers also better learn a different profession because they will not be psychologists for long.

As a student, you may be tempted to dry-lab because an assignment is due and you have not completed it. Don't do it! Late assignments cause lowered grades, but contrived results cause class dismissals and terrible letters of recommendation. Professional scientists are totally intolerant of such behavior.

---

*Note here that I am using the term *relevant* in quite a different way from the way it is used by many people. I mean relevant to science, not "relevant" to faddish topics. Sometimes topics that are "relevant" in the latter sense are the least relevant in the former sense.

† This term has nothing to do with the drinking habits of the experimenter.

Back in the early 1900s, a biologist named Kammerer[1] attempted to demonstrate that acquired characteristics could be inherited—a concept antithetical to Darwinian evolution. He claimed that he had kept generations of fire salamanders on black soil. He reported not only that the salamanders, which are normally black with yellow spots, showed increasingly smaller spots over generations, but also that this reduction was passed on by inheritance. A second researcher, who doubted these claims, added the time required to bring forth the number of generations Kammerer reported and found that the total time was considerably longer than Kammerer had been at work. Other scientists also began to demand explanations until, after seven years, two leading scientists were allowed to examine some specimens. They found injections of India ink. Kammerer admitted that his results "had plainly been 'improved' post mortem with India ink." He then promptly committed suicide.

Today investigators generally take less drastic action when they are caught tampering with their data, but it is still an extremely unpleasant experience. Recently an established investigator became the director of a well-known ESP laboratory. One ESP experiment used electronic equipment to record rats' responses. Apparently, the new lab director was under extreme pressure to produce positive results from the experiment, for one day an equipment technician found that some wires had been removed from the device that recorded non-ESP responses. The young lab director eventually admitted to having changed the wiring in order to produce the desired effect. He is no longer the director of the lab and will undoubtedly have a problem finding employment as an experimental psychologist in any capacity. Of necessity, scientists are unforgiving of such behavior in their colleagues.

The most dastardly deed in science is to add noise to the body of knowledge. If you do bad research, people can and will ignore it, but if you pretend that you have done good research when you have not, you will retard the expansion of the body of knowledge. Others will come along and attempt to build their research on yours, only to discover eventually that something is wrong. They must then waste their time fixing the foundation and possibly rebuilding the whole structure. The longer such cheating goes undetected, the greater the eventual waste of science's resources.

If undetected, the cheating of science can also lead to the cheating of society. In the late 1930s, for example, a Russian named Lysenko[2] also supported the notion that acquired characteristics could be inherited. He was so adamant about this theory that he falsified a great deal of data. Lysenkoites claimed that they had brought about such miraculous results as transforming wheat into rye, barley, oats, and even cornflowers; beets into cabbage; pine into fir; a tree of the hornbeam group into forest walnut (using doctored photographs as evidence); and even the hatching of cuckoos from eggs laid by warblers.[2]

Lysenko's grossly unethical behavior hurt not only science but society as well. He was personally responsible for the dismissal, exile, and execution of a number of Russian geneticists. He convinced Stalin and

later Khrushchev that his theories were correct and that they should be applied on a large scale in agricultural programs.[3] When later devastating agricultural failures were attributed in part to Lysenko's methods, Lysenko fell, Khrushchev fell, and Russian society suffered.

If this discussion has put fear into your heart, it was supposed to. Fear should not be your major deterrent, however. Your development of respect for the basic processes of science should provide adequate motivation to discourage you from reporting false data.

In order to protect yourself against false accusations (not to mention the value of having data available for further analysis), you should keep the *raw data** from any experiment for a minimum of five years following publication or reporting. It is common for investigators to write to each other requesting copies of the raw data from an experiment for replication or analysis. (It's also appropriate for the original experimenter to ask the requester to pay any copying costs.) It used to be quite a task keeping old data in an orderly form, but modern computers are now very fast, accurate, and neat about printing these records for you.

Falsifying Credentials

If you were to walk up to a friend and say "Would you stand on your head for me?" the response would probably be "Why?" However, if you

---

*The individual measurements of your dependent variable prior to combining them for statistical analysis are your *raw data*. Unlike meat, raw data do not spoil—they just take up room.

were to walk up to another friend and say "I'm doing an experiment. Would you stand on your head for me?" your friend's response is more likely to be "How long?" This difference arises from the fact that our society grants scientists a number of privileges not given to the average citizen. We allow scientists, particularly behavioral scientists, the freedom to experiment because, as a society, we feel that the gains usually outweigh the costs. We also grant scientists a certain amount of prestige and generally respond to them somewhat compliantly.

We not only allow scientists to manipulate the lives of those around them, but sometimes we also support them in this effort by our tax money. However, we are also capable of taking away these privileges if we believe that the gains no longer outweigh the costs. Requiring professional credentials of experimenters is one way we police ourselves. Consequently, to prove to other scientists that you are a qualified investigator, you will need to present them with your professional record, usually in the form of a vita or résumé. A résumé is a piece of paper that shows who you are professionally: it lists your educational degrees, your job experience, and your published papers and articles. You use it to get into graduate school, to become professionally certified, or to get a job. Perhaps it should go without saying that this document must be totally accurate. I will say it anyway—*falsifying credentials* is blatant cheating.

Early in my career, I saw a very talented student attempt to get into graduate school using a falsified vita. He had a fine record and great letters of recommendation from his professors, but he listed several papers and articles on his vita that did not exist. When his professors discovered his deception, the student no longer had either a fine record or letters of recommendation; nor is he an experimental psychologist today. Because the agreement between scientists and society is fragile, this type of dishonesty upsets the delicate balance and cannot be tolerated.

I hope that this discussion of blatant cheating was a waste of your time and that you would not have considered doing it in the first place. Yet I believe that such topics must be mentioned early in an experimenter's training. Doing psychology experiments can be fun, but the real purpose of experimentation is building science. Those who are not willing to follow the rules that make this process an orderly one do not belong in science.

MODERATE CHEATING

Those actions that most investigators find unacceptable but that lead to frowning and scolding rather than banishment can be considered moderate cheating. These actions can take place during the design of an experiment, during the experiment itself, during data analysis, or in experimental reporting.

Experimental Design

In the previous chapter, we discussed experimenter bias as communicated through demand characteristics. If you design your experiment so that the demand characteristics themselves could cause a desired change in the dependent variable and do not attempt to minimize these demand characteristics or even discover them, you are, in a sense, cheating. You can also confound an experiment if you claim to have made a particular variable into a control variable when, in fact, this variable systematically changed with your independent variable. In some non-laboratory experiments such *confounding* is difficult to control, but in many cases we can legitimately call this situation cheating.

For example, suppose a college instructor wants to find out if the rate at which he lectures in his introductory psychology class has an effect on his students' attentiveness. He designs the following experiment. On some days he will attempt to speak at a slow pace, on other days he will speak at a moderate pace, and on others at a fast pace. He

will then measure attentiveness by recording the level of background noise and by videotaping selected students. Such an experiment would be very easy to bias.* A biased instructor could change not only his pace but also the degree of liveliness with which he talks about the topic or perhaps the places in the room from which he lectures. Such nonverbal cues could easily confound the independent variable, whether or not the confounding was intended by the instructor.

One way to minimize the chances of cheating would be to design the experiment so that a set of colleagues with little investment in any given outcome would rate each lecture in terms of the possible confounding variables. The experimenter could then collect data only from those lectures with equivalent ratings. Moderate cheating in the form of experimenter bias would not necessarily occur in the first design, of course, but the second design would be more convincing since such bias would be less likely to occur.

Collecting Data

You can also cheat while collecting your data, especially if you need to use human judgment to determine what response the subject has made. In the experiment we just discussed, for example, the experimenter wants to classify the subject's behavior as attentive or inattentive in order to record the percentage of time spent in attentive versus inattentive listening. Suppose one student sits scribbling with her pencil on a piece of paper. Is she taking notes or doodling? Another student has his eyes closed. Is he concentrating or sleeping? We can classify the behaviors quite differently depending upon our bias. If the experimenter who holds the bias is also doing the classifying, the potential problems are obvious.

WHICH STUDENT IS THE ATTENTIVE ONE?

*I know. I was the instructor in this experiment![4]

In order to avoid this form of cheating, the experimenter might construct a standard checklist of attentive and inattentive behaviors and have several judges observe the tapes and independently classify the subjects' behaviors. It would even be possible to keep judges blind to the pace the instructor had used for the tape being observed. Such precautions will decrease the possibility of cheating, either intentional or unintentional.

Bias can sometimes occur even in experiments in which measurement of responses seems straightforward. Suppose an experiment calls for subjects to try to move a stick in order to line up a marker with a moving target. After every ten-second interval, the experimenter must quickly read a pointer on a voltmeter dial and reset it. (The farther the marker is from the target, the more quickly the pointer moves across the dial.) Depending upon the characteristics of the dial, this task can be quite difficult since the needle seldom falls directly on an index line. The experimenter could easily make biased judgments about the location of the pointer on the dial. In this experiment, experimenters had to read the dial over 15,000 times, giving rise to the possibility that small inconsistencies in reading the instrument would eventually bias experimental results. Thus, whenever biased experimenters must use judgment to interpret a subject's response, they should devise procedures to ensure that the judgment will be made accurately.

Data Analysis

You must also avoid cheating in analyzing your data. Although we have not discussed the use of statistical analysis, you should be aware that statistical tests are usually computed to determine whether a particular result is likely to be a real effect or whether it is due to chance. These statistical tests can be used only when certain assumptions can be approximated. Using the test when the *test assumptions* are grossly violated is cheating.

For example, the most frequently used statistical tests require that the underlying distribution be approximately normal. A normal distribution is a bell-shaped symmetrical distribution that you are probably familiar with. While a small violation of this assumption usually does not totally invalidate such a test, some investigators continue to use one of these tests when their distributions in no way resemble a normal distribution. As an experimenter, it is up to you to know what assumptions your statistical test requires and how likely it is that you will make an error if you fail to meet one or more of these assumptions.

When analyzing your data you may discover that while most of the subjects seem to be showing the predicted experimental effect, several do not show the effect. At this point, you can do nothing about these renegade subjects.* Obviously, if you could throw out data from all of the subjects who fail to show an expected result, you would never do an

---

*Unless you are specifically interested in investigating individual differences.

experiment that failed to support your predictions! For this reason, you must be very careful about eliminating subjects from an analysis based on their performance on the dependent variable. And you should never eliminate them based on their different responses to the levels of the independent variable.

You can eliminate subjects for failing to meet some overall performance level on the dependent variable only if you determine this performance level prior to collecting the data, if you can logically defend it, and if you specify the performance level in your experimental report. As an illustration, suppose you were interested in the effects of noise on a subject's ability to perform a typing task. Prior to starting the experiment, you might decide that you will exclude data from all subjects who fail to type at least ten words per minute in the absence of noise. Your logic might be that these subjects are such poor typists to begin with that even if noise has a detrimental effect on typing, they would not show the effect. Or you might argue that you are interested in the effect of noise on experienced typists and that a speed of less than ten words per minute indicates that the subject is not an experienced typist. However, if you do not have a logical argument for eliminating subjects based on a predetermined dependent-variable performance level, you should not do it.

You are much safer in eliminating subjects on a basis other than performance on your dependent variable. Again, however, such criteria should be set prior to the experiment and should be specified when you report the results. For example, you might be having subjects search through an array of letters to report which letter is printed in red ink. In this case, you might exclude subjects who cannot pass an acuity test or a color-blindness test prior to the experiment.

Reporting Results

Suppose you have analyzed your experiment and are now ready to report the results. Usually you will want to put some of your results into a graph. (We will discuss some rules to follow in making a graph in Chapter 10.) People have written books on how to lie by *distorting graphs*.[5] For example, an experimenter could blow up one of the graph's axes in order to make a tiny effect look like a gigantic effect or possibly distort the scale on one axis so that the function being displayed changes shape. If you are a creative person, you can find all sorts of ways to make crummy results look good. Obviously, such behavior does nothing to advance science and so is considered cheating.

One other form of moderate cheating is *piecemeal reporting* of experimental results. Whereas research must progress one experiment at a time, you should not report research in this way. Several decades ago the typical journal article in psychology reported the results of a single experiment. In recent years, however, the field of psychology has grown by such leaps and bounds that there has been a literature explosion. So many people are doing so many experiments that the process of keeping current with experimental advances is nearly impossible. For this reason, few journals will accept a report of a single experiment unless it makes an unusually large contribution by itself. Usually, you should report the results of your experimental research program as an integrated series of experiments. With this procedure, the growth of knowledge becomes much more efficient and orderly and readers are spared the task of reorienting themselves to the research, rereading introduction and procedure sections with each experiment, and integrating fragmented research into a coherent structure. In today's "publish or perish" world, an investigator can be tempted to do piecemeal reporting

A LITERATURE EXPLOSION

in order to accumulate publications. However, in the end, such behavior does nothing to improve either the investigator's reputation or the body of scientific knowledge.

ACCEPTED CHEATING

Although the term *accepted cheating* sounds self-contradictory, it is sometimes necessary to "lie" to the reader of a research report in order to communicate efficiently. Research is usually a sloppy process, yet when you read an experimental report it sounds as if the investigator proceeded in a systematic, orderly fashion at all times.* Don't believe it! Rarely does a researcher's mind work in the totally logical manner reflected in his or her report. Experimenters make many decisions based on hunches or gut-level intuitions. They make false starts based on bad guesses. They do experiments the right way for the wrong reasons or the wrong way for the right reasons.

Unfortunately, many students become turned off to experimental psychology because they think it is dry and unexciting, when in most cases it is actually an exciting, disorderly, haphazard treasure hunt. You know little about experimentation until you try your first experiment.†

---

*A charmingly written article on the sometimes haphazard process of research is B. F. Skinner's *A case history in scientific method.*[6]

†It's kind of like making love: reading about it is a poor substitute for doing it.

The most obvious reason for cleaning up an experimental report is to save time and space. While it might be fun to read about all of your colleague's mistakes, you do not have the time and journals do not have the space to allow us the luxury. The experimental report is designed to convey information efficiently, not entertain the reader.*

Leaving Things Out

One way of cleaning up your experimental report is to *leave out experiments and analyses*.† Suppose you had a bad day when you designed the third experiment in a series, or you had a bad intuition, or you were temporarily confused. Nobody else is interested in the condition of your life, your viscera, or your head. So you blew the experiment. I don't want to read about it. You don't want to write about it. So don't. Science loses nothing, I lose nothing, and you save face.

Not only is it acceptable to leave out whole experiments if they add nothing to the report, but at times it is also proper to ignore the details of some data analyses. Perhaps there were a number of ways to analyze your data, and you did them all. While you should probably report that you did the analyses, you need give details of only those that are most representative and convey the most information.‡

Reorganizing

Especially when doing exploratory research, you may find that the outcome of an experiment shows that it should not have been the first experiment in the series. You may find it desirable to back up and do some preliminary experiments. In such cases, you need not tell the reader that "due to misjudgment and lack of foresight on the experimenter's part, the following experiments are out of order." You may report them in the most logical order, whether or not this order matches the order in which you did them. Data are data, and you should report them as efficiently as possible, as long as bending the truth does not bend the science.

Reformulating

Finally, an accepted method of cheating in an experimental report is to *reformulate the theory* underlying an experiment. Occasionally you will do an experiment for some reason and later discover a better reason for having done it. Or perhaps you will discover that somebody else has done an experiment that casts a different light on one you are conducting. In this case, you will have to determine how your contribution to the body of knowledge will best fit with the new information. Unfortu-

---

* A lot of textbook writers think this, too. They never have any fun!
† Or else put them in a footnote. Nobody reads footnotes.
‡ Note that I am not endorsing the practice of conducting a multitude of tests and then picking and choosing only those that yield significant results. In this case, you are distorting the level of significance (Chapter 9).

nately, there will be times when your theory does not fit at all and you will have to go back to the drawing board. Often, however, you will be able to fit your experiment into the revised theory by changing your emphasis or reinterpreting your results. In reporting your results, you need not burden the reader with obsolete theory. Again, your major ethical consideration should be whether you are adding to the body of knowledge in an efficient manner.

In this chapter we have by no means exhausted all of the ethical questions that you will face as an experimenter. In some cases, you will find it difficult to decide whether a particular action is fair to science. When a problem comes up, you may wish to discuss it with colleagues, who may be able to raise points and suggest alternatives that you have not considered. In the end, though, the decision is yours. If you apply the principle that ethical actions are those that aid in the efficient growth of the body of knowledge, you will never be a blatant cheater and seldom be a moderate cheater.

SUMMARY

Since science is a growing body of knowledge, any action that retards the efficient expansion of that body of knowledge is unethical. We can be less than totally truthful with science in a number of ways. We can blatantly cheat by *dry-labbing* results or by falsifying our credentials. We can also cheat in more moderate ways—by failing to control confounding variables in the design of an experiment, for example, or by misclassifying responses and misreading instruments during collection of our data. During data analysis, failing to meet test assumptions and inappropriately eliminating subjects are forms of moderate cheating. Cheating in experimental reporting includes distorting graphs and reporting a series of experiments as piecemeal reports. For the sake of efficiency, it is acceptable to write up experimental reports in a form that does not exactly parallel our experiment. For example, we can leave out experiments and analyses from a report if they do not add to the report, or we can reorder experiments and reformulate theory if these actions increase the efficiency of the experimental report.

REFERENCES

1. Ley, W. *Salamanders and other wonders.* New York: Viking Press, 1955.
2. Lerner, I. M. *Heredity, evolution, and society.* San Francisco: Freeman, 1968.
3. Medvedev, Z. A. *The rise and fall of T. D. Lysenko* (I. M. Lerner, trans.). New York: Columbia University Press, 1969.
4. Grobe, R. P., Pettibone, T. J., & Martin, D. W. Effectiveness of lecture pace on noise level in a university classroom. *Journal of Educational Research,* 1973, *67,* 73–75.
5. Huff, D. *How to lie with statistics.* New York: Norton, 1954.
6. Skinner, B. F. A case history in scientific method. In S. Koch (Ed.), *Psychology: A study of a science.* New York: McGraw-Hill, 1959.

How to Choose Independent and Dependent Variables 6

> We believe that a concept has no meaning beyond that obtained from the operations on which it is based.*

We discussed a general model of an experiment in Chapter 1 and how to get experimental ideas in Chapter 2. In Chapter 3 you probably learned more about doing a literature search than you wished to know. We considered subject ethics and science ethics respectfully and respectively in Chapters 4 and 5. Now it's time we got to work doing what experimental psychologists are supposed to do—experiments.

In this chapter, we will consider two decisions that have to be made when planning any psychology experiment, from the simplest to the most complex. We need to choose the independent and dependent variables.

CHOOSING AN INDEPENDENT VARIABLE

Recall from Chapter 1 that the independent variable is the one that the experimenter manipulates. Since the whole purpose of any experiment is to find the effect of the independent variable on the subject's behavior, choosing this variable is about the most important decision you have to make. At first blush it may seem that the decision should be rather straightforward. And for some experiments it is. For example, if you want to know whether people press a button in response to a light more

*Garner, W. R., Hake, H. W., & Eriksen, C. W. Operationalism and the concept of perception. *Psychological Review,* 1956, *63*, 149–159.

quickly when a tone is given as a warning signal, the independent variable is rather obvious—the presence or absence of the tone. If, however, you want to find out if children are more aggressive after exposure to violent versus nonviolent TV programs, the independent variable (violence) may be tougher to define. What constitutes violent TV? Is "Monday Night Football" violent? Are "Roadrunner" cartoons violent? Is "Wild Kingdom" violent? Not everyone would agree on a particular definition of violent TV.

The problem here is that there is a difference in precision between what the general public will accept in defining a term and what experimental psychologists will accept. Experimental psychologists require an *operational definition* of the independent and dependent variables. This means that they must specify the operations they would go through to determine if a TV program were violent and outline the specific steps they would take to classify TV programs.

For example, if you were conducting our TV experiment, you could operationalize the concept of a violent TV program by showing each program to a randomly chosen group of 100 people and requiring that 75% of them indicate a program is violent before you operationally define it as violent. Another alternative would be to devise a checklist with such items as: "Is there physical contact of an aggressive nature?" "Has an illegal act taken place?" "Did one person act so as to make another feel inferior?" Perhaps you would require that each program have at least two out of ten such items checked "yes" in order for it to be

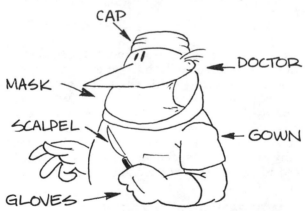

CAP

MASK

SCALPEL

GLOVES

DOCTOR

GOWN

OPERATIONAL DEFINITIONS

considered violent. Again, such a procedure would specify exactly what operations any other experimenter must carry out in order to meet your operational definition of violent TV.

Psychology researchers have more difficulty agreeing on operational definitions than do physical scientists.* Galileo did not have to

---

*A physicist first used the term *operational definition*. However, in the physical sciences operational definitions are usually so widely accepted that physical scientists spend considerably less time agonizing over them.

ponder over a definition for mass prior to determining whether objects that have different masses fall at the same speed in a vacuum. Yet a great many important psychological questions require complex operational definitions: Do people whose mothers were affectionate make more successful marriage partners? Do students learn more from popular professors? Does a worker's morale affect work output? Does anxiety cause depression? Prior to doing an experiment to answer any of these questions, you would need operational definitions for the terms *affectionate, popular, morale,* and *anxiety.* Try making up operational definitions for these terms; you will quickly see the psychology researcher's challenge.

Choosing the Range of Your Independent Variable

Once you have defined your independent variable, you still have to choose the range of the variable. The *range* is the difference between the highest and lowest level of the variable you choose. For example, suppose we decided to define violent TV using our group of 100 people to classify each program as violent or nonviolent. We could choose to use two levels of violence in our experiment—those programs classified as violent by 100% of the people and those that nobody thought were violent. These two levels of the independent variable give us the largest possible range.

On the other hand, we might have chosen the programs rated violent by over 50% of the people as violent and those rated violent by less than 50% as nonviolent. These levels would obviously create a much smaller range.

How do we determine what the range should be? Unfortunately I can't give you any hard and fast rules for making this decision, for it is as much an art as a science. However, there are some guidelines that you might find useful.

Be realistic.   First, you should try to choose a range that is *realistic* in that it is similar to the levels found in the situation you will be generalizing to. You should avoid "sledgehammer" effects caused by setting the levels of the independent variable at such extremes that you are certain to find a difference in behavior. Some of the early medical research on marijuana was plagued by sledgehammer effects. In some cases, experimenters gave mice the human equivalent of a truckload per day of marijuana! The experimenters got impressive but impractical results.

A "SLEDGEHAMMER" EFFECT

Select a range that shows effect.   Within realistic limits, you should have a range that is large enough to show an effect of the independent variable on the dependent variable if such an effect exists. For example, if you were interested in the effect of room temperature on typing speed and you chose temperatures of 23° C. and 25° C.,* you might conclude falsely that room temperature has no effect on typing speed.

Real-world† experimental situations require special attention to choosing a large enough range because the experimenter does not always have complete control over the levels of the independent variable.

---

* For those of you who refuse to be converted to converting Celsius, 73° F. and 77° F.

† I use the term *real world* to refer to nonlaboratory experiments designed to find answers to applied problems, not to imply that most people in universities are unreal. People who live in ivory towers shouldn't throw snipes.

You can choose an approximate level, but the actual level may vary from trial to trial. In the lecture-pace experiment we described earlier, the instructor (me) attempted to vary the lecture pace by speaking at a slow, medium, or fast rate. The levels I attempted to achieve were 100, 125, and 150 syllables per minute. Since I am not a machine that can be set at a particular speaking rate, I was bound to produce some variability around the desired levels. To determine my actual rate, we recorded the lectures and counted the number of syllables per second. Fortunately, the fastest lecture at the slow pace was still slower than the slowest lecture at the medium pace so there was no overlap of levels. If I had chosen a smaller range, however, I would have had less chance of producing these reliable differences among the levels of the independent variable. Thus, in some nonlaboratory experiments you must remember to make the range large enough that differences in the levels of the independent variable are not covered up by the uncontrolled variability of that variable.

Do a pilot experiment.   Determining the best range for an experiment is to some extent guesswork. In some cases, you may find experiments using the same independent variable you are planning to use that can give you an idea about an appropriate range. However, if your experiment is original and nobody else has used an independent variable similar to yours, you may choose to do a *pilot experiment.** A pilot experiment is a small-scale version of the experiment you are planning, done so you can iron out any problems before you proceed. Since you need not report the results of this experiment, you may break some of the rules of experimentation. For example, you might cajole your friends into serving as subjects, and you might even serve as your own subject.

SUBJECT FOR A
PILOT EXPERIMENT

*I suppose the term *pilot* in this case is used in the sense of "guiding through unknown places," as when a ship's pilot comes on board to steer a vessel through unknown waters. Experimentation, too, often proceeds through uncharted waters.

You can also change the levels of your independent variable halfway through a trial, stop the experiment, or do only part of the experiment, depending on what you learn as you proceed.

While doing a pilot experiment you will sometimes find that what looked good on paper just does not work. I once discovered during a pilot experiment that a supposedly simple experiment I had designed required at least three experimenters to operate the equipment, for example. The pilot experiment may also help you determine whether the levels of your independent variable are what you expected. Levels that seem realistic during the planning stage of an experiment may seem unrealistic to the laboratory subject. By having a trial run, you can change an obviously inappropriate range of the independent variable before investing a great amount of time and effort in the experiment.

Although searching the literature and doing pilot experiments can give you some idea of an appropriate range for your independent variable, in the end you still have to make your best guess. If you turn out to be right, you can claim good judgment. If you are wrong, it's bad luck.

CHOOSING A DEPENDENT VARIABLE

As we know from Chapter 1, the dependent variable is some measure of the subject's behavior. We saw that there are an infinite number of things we could choose to measure. In selecting our dependent variable, we must decide what we will measure.

Operational Definitions Again

Let's go back to the question "Will violent TV shows cause a change in a child's aggressiveness?" In this experiment, we clearly want to measure aggressiveness, but again we will need an operational definition of aggressiveness so that we can determine whether a child's behavior changes after viewing violent TV shows.

One way to develop an operational definition would be to have a panel of judges watch a movie of each child in a free-play situation and then rate the child's aggressiveness on a seven-point scale. Or we could tell each child several stories about other children in frustrating situations and ask the child what he or she would do in each situation. We could then use the number of "direct-attack" responses as a measure of aggressiveness. Another alternative would be to observe children as they play with a selection of toys we had previously classified as aggressive—such as guns, tanks, and knives—or nonaggressive—such as trucks, tools, and dolls. We could then measure the percentage of time that the child played with each type of toy. You can undoubtedly think of many other behaviors that would be an indication of a child's aggressiveness.

With dependent variables, not only do we have to be concerned with determining an operational definition, but we have to know whether the measurement is *reliable* and *valid*.

Reliability and Validity

A measuring instrument is perfectly reliable if we get exactly the same result when we repeat a measurement a number of times. The more variable the results, the less reliable is the measuring instrument. A rubber ruler, for example, would not be very reliable. It might measure a tabletop at 18 inches one time and 31 inches the next time. In order to find out how reliable the ruler is, we would have to measure a number of objects at least two times and see how the results correlate (Chapter 1). If the result of the first measurement is similar to that of the second, then there is high correlation and we can assume that the measuring instrument is reliable. If there is low correlation, then we would know that the instrument is not very reliable.

To use our violent-TV example, we might show the same set of movies of each child's behavior to a second panel of judges and compare the aggressiveness ratings given by the two panels. If the panels gave similar ratings, we can feel more confident that ratings taken from a panel of judges are reliable.

Validity refers to whether we are measuring what we want to measure. Suppose we have a wooden ruler marked as 12 inches long, but it is really 24 inches long because each inch on the ruler actually measures 2 inches. In this case, we could measure the tabletop many times and the ruler would indicate 11 inches every time. We have a reliable

A NONAGGRESSIVE TOY?

measuring instrument, but, of course, the measurement is wrong because we claim that we are measuring in inches when in fact we are not. Thus, we also need to know if our measuring instruments are *valid*—that is, if they measure in the same units as a standard measuring device known to be valid.

In establishing our operational definition of aggressiveness, for example, suppose we had decided to measure the percentage of time each child spent playing with aggressive versus nonaggressive toys. If our stopwatch were working correctly, this measurement would probably be quite reliable since we would get about the same reading when we timed the behavior a second time. However, people might argue that our measure is not a valid measure of aggressiveness. They might claim that children tend to play with toys that they already know how to use. Since they have seen guns and tanks and knives used on violent TV, they choose those toys to play with. Or they might claim that children can use trucks and tools and dolls in aggressive ways as well as nonaggressive ways. To convince them that your measure is valid, you would have to compare it to some standard that you both agree is a valid measure of aggressiveness. If your measuring instrument agreed with the standard, then you could call it a valid instrument.

Directly Observable Dependent Variables

The least controversial dependent variables are those we can observe directly. Direct observation is possible when the behavior we are interested in can be measured directly; in such cases we do not have to infer the existence of a behavior through measuring one of its by-products. Examples of directly observable dependent variables are response speed, response accuracy, and response magnitude. Even with these fairly straightforward measures, however, we should recognize that we are limiting ourselves to measuring only one aspect of the subject's behavior and that we are by no means measuring the subject's complete response to manipulation of the independent variable.

Single dependent variables.   Suppose we want to know whether a subject will respond more quickly to a bright light than to a dim light when pushing a button. We would probably start a clock when the light occurred and stop the clock when the button was pressed. We should recognize that we are measuring only one characteristic of the response. We could have chosen any number of other characteristics—how subjects press the button, for example. Does one subject move her finger from the side of the button on one trial and from directly over the button on the next? On one trial, does she miss the button on the first try? On another trial, does she hit the button lightly at first and then mash it down? From this diverse set of responses, we chose to measure only one characteristic of the response: time from light onset to button depression. In other words, we selected a *single dependent variable.*

The single dependent variable we choose may or may not be the appropriate measure to take. For example, suppose we ask a subject to use a pencil to trace the outline of a star while looking at the star in a mirror. Since the mirror reverses everything, most subjects find this task very tough on the first few trials. Suppose we want to measure a subject's improvement from Trial 1 to Trial 10 on this task. What dependent variable would best reflect this improvement?

The standard dependent variable used in these experiments is the number of times the subject's tracing crosses the outline of the star. Figure 6-1 shows the tracings from two fictitious subjects that we will sagaciously call Subject 1 and Subject 2. On Trial 1, Subject 1 crossed the boundary 20 times, compared to 6 times on Trial 10. For this subject, the dependent variable reflects the expected improvement in performance. But look at Subject 2. This subject crossed the outline 14 times on each of the two trials. Our dependent variable indicates that Subject 2 did not improve in mirror-tracing performance. Do you believe this conclusion?

The basic problem is that even when we use a directly observable dependent variable such as number of border crossings, we must be concerned with validity. Border-crossing behavior is only one possible measure of mirror-tracing performance. Is it a valid measure? Other dependent variables might better reflect overall mirror-tracing performance. As an alternative, we could have measured the total length of the tracing and determined what percentage fell within the borders of the star. Or we could have measured the area between the border and the tracing for each trial. Or we could have timed the subjects to find out whether they were tracing the star more quickly by the tenth trial.

Multiple dependent variables. One way to improve the chances that we will be using a valid dependent variable is to use *multiple dependent variables.* In fact, in some areas of experimental psychology it is considered quite inappropriate to report only one dependent measure.

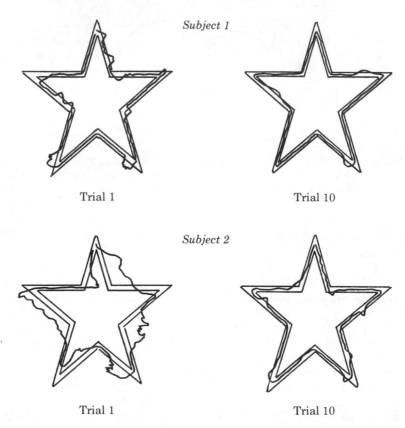

Figure 6–1.   Star-tracing performance of two subjects on Trials 1 and 10.

For example, many types of research use choice reaction time as a dependent measure. Choice reaction time is the time it takes a subject to give one of several responses when one of several stimuli* occurs. Naturally, if subjects wish to make as few errors as possible, they must respond rather slowly. If they are willing to be less accurate, they can respond more quickly. This speed-accuracy tradeoff makes it necessary that both speed and accuracy be reported as dependent variables. If we are interested in a subject's overall level of performance, one measure is useless without the other. For this reason, the better journals will not accept articles that report only speed or only accuracy of a choice-reaction-time response.

Compound dependent variables.   While it is generally a good idea to report as many aspects of the subject's behavior as possible, this practice can make interpreting the results much more difficult. Suppose

---

*Since I haven't used the term *stimuli* before, I should point out that *stimulus* is singular and *stimuli* is plural. It is time to expand your chant: "This stimulus is, this datum is; these stimuli are, these data are." Got that?

we have four dependent variables: one measure shows great improvement across conditions, two stay the same, and one decreases slightly. In order to say anything about the overall change in behavior, we need a way of combining our single dependent variables into a *compound dependent variable* that will give some indication of overall performance.

A number of areas in experimental psychology use compound dependent variables. One area of research is concerned with how we organize words in order to remember them. Suppose I presented you with a list of 16 words composed of 4 words from each of 4 categories. If I presented the 16 words to you in a mixed-up order and had you recall them in any order you like, you would tend to recall them by category. Figure 6-2 shows a typical list of responses. In order to evaluate the results, it would be useful to have some way of representing how organized the recalled list is. One way to present the results would be to count the number of clusters in the list, where a *cluster* is defined as two or more words from the same category occurring together. A problem with this measure is that fewer clusters would not necessarily indicate successful recall through clustering; a list could have fewer clusters because the subject recalled the words in a more organized way or simply because the subject recalled fewer words. Consequently, experimenters developed a compound dependent variable called the *ratio of repetition* as a measure of organization.[1] Figure 6-2 shows how to calculate a ratio of repetition for the list shown there. You can see that this number gets larger the more words there are in a cluster, the fewer clusters there are, and the fewer words recalled. Thus, it gives some indication of how organized a list is. While the ratio of repetition is an example of combining several separate measures into a compound dependent variable, its validity has been attacked by a number of other researchers[2] who have proposed their own measures. The controversy continues.

A second type of compound dependent variable combines several instances of a single measure. These instances are taken at different

Clusters	Order of Recall		
1	⌈ perch ⌊ trout		
2	⌈ maple oak ⌊ pine	$RR = \dfrac{\text{Number of clustered words} - \text{Number of clusters}}{\text{Number of words recalled} - 1}$		
3	⌈ bass ⌊ tuna		
4	⌈ hammer pliers ⌊ screwdriver	$RR = \dfrac{12 - 5}{13 - 1} \;=\; \dfrac{7}{12} \;=\; .58$	
5	⌈ horse ⌊ cow		
	saw		

Figure 6–2. Calculating a ratio of repetition for a typical list of words.

times or under different conditions. *Percent savings* is one such dependent variable used in memory research. Suppose, for example, you learned to ride a bicycle when you were 10 years old and then did not touch a bike again until you were 40. We could now have you relearn bike riding, practicing for a number of trials until you could stay up for a minute without touching the ground. Suppose it took you seven trials to do this. We could then compare this number to the number of trials it would take a second 40-year-old who had never ridden a bike to stay up for a minute. Suppose it took this person 14 trials. We could then calculate the percent of trials you saved by having learned to ride at an earlier age:

$$\% \text{ saved} = \frac{\text{Number of trials to learn} - \text{Number of trials to relearn}}{\text{Number of trials to learn}} \times 100.$$

In our example:

$$\% \text{ saved} = \frac{14 - 7}{14} \times 100 = 50\%.$$

Through this type of compound dependent variable, you can use a single number to show the effect of a change caused by the independent variable (past bike-riding experience).

It may not be clear to you yet how these compound dependent variables were derived or why they are appropriate measures, but you will become familiar with many others if you do research in certain areas of psychology. You may even find yourself making up your own compound dependent variables someday.

Indirect Dependent Variables

It is sometimes impossible to directly observe the behavior you are interested in, yet we know that the ROT (repeatable, observable, testable) test of science requires that the behavior we are studying be publicly observable. How then can we do scientific research in such areas as emotion, learning, or intelligence? We need an indirect dependent variable that changes along with the internal behavior we are interested in.

Physiological measures.   Probably the most popular type of indirect dependent variables are *physiological measures,* which are based on the idea that if the behavior itself is a private event, such as an emotion, perhaps the physiology of the body will change along with the private event. Since modern technology allows us to observe changes in the physiology of the body, experimenters use these changes to infer what the private event must have been.

Of course, when we use physiological measures to infer internal states, we are assuming that a unique physiological pattern accurately reflects an internal state. For example, a polygraph or lie detector measures four physiological processes—respiratory rate, heart rate, blood pressure, and galvanic skin response.* The operator then uses these measures to determine whether the accused was telling the truth. Some people doubt whether the assumption behind using physiological measures is correct. For this reason, the results of a lie-detector test are admissible evidence in most courts only if both the plaintiff and the defendant agree to their use.

Other physiological measures have become popular as researchers claim that they give an indication of some emotional state. They then lose favor as other investigators show that they can get the same type of physiological change with a different internal state. For example, an investigator named Hess at one point claimed that the diameter of a person's pupil increases when he or she is thinking pleasant thoughts and decreases when the person is thinking about unpleasant things. For a while, the Madison Avenue advertising tycoons were so impressed that they used pupillary responses to choose magazine advertisements. Other investigators have since found that the diameter of the pupil is perhaps a better indication of the amount of information the person is processing rather than the emotions the person is feeling.[3] Pupillometricians are no longer welcome on Madison Avenue.

Recently investigators have claimed that the characteristics of a person's voice can be used for "psychological stress evaluation." By tape recording a voice, slowing it down, and measuring certain aspects of vocal frequencies, these investigators believe that they can tell when a person is under great stress, such as they would be when lying. These claims have yet to be proven.

Physiological measures do offer some hope as indirect dependent variables, but at present there is some doubt about exactly what internal state each reflects.

Behavioral measures. Some *behavioral measures* are also used as indirect independent variables. As with physiological measures, some investigators claim that changes in the way a person performs a behavioral task can reflect the person's internal state. For example, one experimental finding shows that people and other animals will change their rate of response when they are expecting a strong shock to occur.[4]

Experimenters have also used indirect behavioral measures to measure the amount of mental processing required by a particular task. For instance, you might wish to know how much processing a memory task requires during a single trial. The usual dependent variable would be some measure of the amount of information the subject retained, such as the number of items recalled or recognized. However, this measure tells you only what the terminal performance was and gives you no idea what the ongoing processing requirements of the task have been. In

---

* In case you are not familiar with the term *galvanic skin response,* it is not a rash caused by handling too many garbage cans. It is a measure of how well the skin will carry a small electric current. Although not technically accurate, the reasoning goes something like this: since wet skin carries electric current better than dry skin, a person who is "in a sweat" has a different galvanic skin response from one who is "cool and calm."

order to get some idea of ongoing processing, you might require subjects to respond to a second task while performing the first. For example, you might have subjects push a button whenever a light comes on at the same time they are learning, remembering, and recalling a list of words. Investigators have found that the time it takes subjects to respond to the light reflects the number of words they are remembering.[2,5] In addition, subjects respond more slowly as more words are being presented and speed up again as they recall words. Figure 6-3 shows an idealized version of this result.

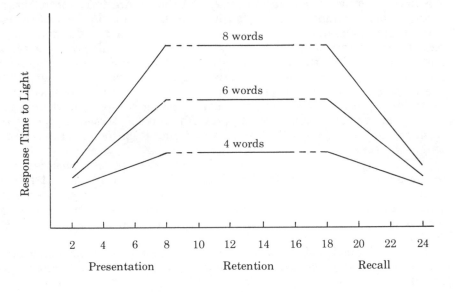

Number of Seconds into Trial

Figure 6–3. An idealized version of the time it takes to respond to a light during the various stages of a memory task. During presentation, the experimenter reads either four, six, or eight words to the subject. The subject retains these words for eight seconds and then recalls them. At one of 12 points in a trial, a light may flash to which the subject pushes a button. The response time to the light appears to reflect the amount of processing required by the memory task.

As with other indirect dependent variables, this dual-task method is based on certain assumptions. One assumption is that people have a rather fixed capacity for processing information, so that the more they use this limited capacity to process the memory task, the less they have available for processing the light-response task. The less residual processing capacity available, the slower will be the subject's response to the light. So, like Archimedes,* who argued that the water overflowing

---

*Archimedes is the fellow your science teachers love to tell you about. He ran naked through the streets of Athens shouting "Eureka! Eureka! I have found it!" upon discovering that he could determine the volume of the king's crown by submerging it in his bathtub and finding out how much water spilled out.

the bathtub reflected the volume of the king's crown, these investigators argue that the processing requirements of the memory task, combined with the processing needed for the light-response task, cause our limited processing capacity to overflow.* This degrades the performance of the light-response task (slows the reaction time) and allows us to infer, by looking at the performance of the light task, the amount of processing the memory task is using.

As with indirect physiological variables, most researchers do not believe that indirect behavioral dependent variables, such as dual-task measures, are the same as directly measuring the internal events. However, they are a valuable tool for getting some idea of the nature of these unobservable behaviors.

SUMMARY

In choosing an independent variable for your experiment, you must first specify an *operational definition* of the variable so that other experimenters will be able to go through the same operations when they conduct similar experiments. It is also important to choose the levels of your independent variable so that the *range* is large enough to show the experimental effect but small enough to be realistic. A trial run, or *pilot experiment,* will sometimes help you in this decision.

The dependent variable must also be operationally defined. In addition, we must be able to show that the dependent variable is *reliable* and *valid.* It is reliable if the same result is obtained every time a measurement is taken. It is valid if the measurement agrees with a commonly accepted standard. *Directly observable dependent variables* are relatively easy to measure, but it is sometimes difficult to decide which *single dependent variable* to use. Some areas of research require that *multiple dependent variables* be reported or that dependent variables be combined to form a *compound dependent variable. Indirect dependent variables* are used when the behavior we are interested in is not publicly observable. *Physiological measures* may provide an indication of the subject's internal state, but they are often difficult to interpret. *Behavioral measures* such as dual-task performance also offer the possibility of determining a subject's internal state.

REFERENCES

1. Cofer, C. N., Bruce, D. R., & Reicher, G. M. Clustering in free recall as a function of certain methodological variations. *Journal of Experimental Psychology,* 1966, *71,* 858–866.
2. Martin, D. W., Marston, P. T., & Kelly, R. T. Measurement of organizational processes within memory stages. *Journal of Experimental Psychology,* 1973, *98,* 387–395.
3. Johnson, D. A. Pupillary responses during a short-term memory task: Cognitive processing, arousal, or both? *Journal of Experimental Psychology,* 1971, *90,* 311–318.

*Now you know why some people have trouble chewing gum and walking at the same time. They have small bathtubs!

4. Sachs, D. A., & May, J. G. The presence of a temporal discrimination in the conditioned emotional response with humans. *Journal of Experimental Analysis of Behavior,* 1969, *12,* 1003–1007.
5. Martin, D. W., & Kelly, R. T. Secondary task performance during directed forgetting. *Journal of Experimental Psychology,* 1974, *103,* 1074–1079.

How to Decide 7 on a Within-Subject versus Between-Subjects Design

Humorist Robert Benchley once divided the world into two groups: those who divide the world into two groups, and those who do not.*

Now that you have chosen an independent variable and decided which levels to use, you must decide how you are going to assign subjects to these levels. There are two basic ways to assign subjects: you can expose each subject to all levels of the variable or you can expose each subject to only one level. The former method is called a *within-subject* design

BETWEEN-SUBJECTS DESIGN: EACH SUBJECT IS EXPOSED TO ONLY ONE LEVEL.

*Time Magazine, May 17, 1976.

because the independent variable is manipulated within a single subject; the latter is called a *between-subjects* design because the variable is manipulated between at least two subjects.* Table 7-1 illustrates the two methods of subject assignment for an experiment that has two levels of an independent variable. In the top case each of the ten subjects is assigned to both levels, while in the bottom case a different set of ten subjects is assigned to each level. Each of these designs has certain advantages and disadvantages.

Table 7–1. The assignment of subjects for a within-subject experiment and a between-subjects experiment.

Within-Subject	Independent Variable	
	Level 1	*Level 2*
	Subject 1	Subject 1
	Subject 2	Subject 2
	.	.
	.	.
	.	.
	Subject 10	Subject 10

Between-Subjects	Independent Variable	
	Level 1	*Level 2*
	Subject 1	Subject 11
	Subject 2	Subject 12
	.	.
	.	.
	.	.
	Subject 10	Subject 20

WITHIN-SUBJECT EXPERIMENTS

Although, as you will see later in this chapter, within-subject designs are by no means the best choice for all experiments, they do offer a number of advantages.

Practical Advantages

One practical advantage of a within-subject experiment is immediately obvious from Table 7-1: fewer subjects are required. If N subjects are required to give you an adequate number of data for a within-subject experiment, then N x 2 are required for a two-level between-subjects experiment, N x 3 for a three-level between-subjects experiment, and so on.

---

*Others have called within-subject designs *Treatments* × *Subject* designs or *repeated-measures designs* on the same subjects. Between-subjects designs are sometimes called *separate groups*.

In many cases, increasing the number of subjects substantially increases the total time required for an experiment. For example, if your experiment requires that you pretrain subjects to do a basic task before you expose them to the experimental manipulation, then you will have to pretrain twice as many subjects in a two-level between-subjects experiment. Suppose you want to know if requiring subjects to remember a certain number of words will interfere with their ability to perform a complex tracking task, which in itself takes several hours to learn. If you then added levels to your independent variable (number of words presented for memory), you would add no more pretraining time in a within-subject experiment but you would increase the number of subjects and thereby the pretraining time in a between-subjects experiment.

It is also common to conduct several practice trials at the beginning of an experiment, a practice that also adds time to an experiment the more subjects you have. These practice trials are designed to minimize warm-up effects—that is, a fast improvement during the first few trials as the subject gets into a state of general readiness.

In addition to the inconvenience of using a large number of subjects for a between-subjects experiment, there will also be times when the number of subjects available to you is limited, especially when the subjects must meet certain requirements. For example, you may need pilots, or race-car drivers, or ballet dancers for certain experiments. Or you may want subjects to be afflicted with some disorder like psychosis or color-blindness or left-handedness. In such cases, you may not be able to find enough subjects who meet these requirements to use a between-subjects design and you will need to rely on a within-subject experiment.

Statistical Advantages

In addition to their greater efficiency, within-subject designs can also be preferable for statistical reasons. We will take a brief look at statistics in Chapter 9, but we can mention a few concepts here.

In an inferential statistical test, experimenters attempt to infer whether any differences they find among the data samples collected at the various levels of the independent variable are due to real differences in behavior of some larger population or due to chance. To make this inference, most of these tests compare the differences between the average performance at the two levels with an estimate of how variable the performance is within each of the levels. A statistical test is more likely to call a difference real if the difference between levels is large or if the estimated variability within levels is small. An example will show you how logical this principle is.

Suppose a track-shoe manufacturer wanted to know whether to sell shoes with 7-mm spikes or 13-mm spikes* to the 100-yard-dash† runners

---

* .276 in. and .512 in.
† 91.44 m.

on a men's track team. To test these shoes, he could randomly choose ten men from a college campus to wear one type of shoe and ten additional men from the same campus to wear the other type. The men in the two groups would probably be quite variable in their times to run the dash—from the 300-pound, 38-year-old ex-bartender, to the 125-pound, 19-year-old halfback. Their scores might look something like those in Table 7-2. If you calculate a mean for the two groups, you find that those wearing 7-mm spikes average .5 seconds faster than those wearing 13-mm spikes. Would this difference convince you that the shorter spikes were better for running the 100-yard dash?

Table 7–2. Individual times to run the 100-yard dash for two groups of randomly chosen men.

Subjects Wearing 7-mm Spikes	Time (in Seconds)	Subjects Wearing 13-mm Spikes	Time (in Seconds)
Mike	11.7	Don	15.7
Bob	18.2	Hector	13.4
Homer	12.2	Ron	18.0
George	15.4	Tom	12.8
Harry	15.8	Steve	13.6
Gordon	13.2	Dale	19.0
John	13.7	Pete	16.2
Bill	19.1	Juan	11.9
Randy	12.9	Dan	14.6
Tim	16.0	Paul	18.0

Mean difference = .5 sec.

Now suppose the manufacturers decided to do a second experiment using members of the track team as subjects and randomly assigning them to the 7-mm and 13-mm groups. Their scores might look something like those in Table 7-3. Again there is a .5-second average advantage for the runners wearing the shorter spikes. Would this difference convince you that the shorter spikes were better?

Undoubtedly, you would be more likely to accept the difference found in the second experiment as being a real difference. Because the scores in the second experiment were less variable, you probably feel that the difference found there is less likely to be due entirely to chance variation.

Most of the variability in the scores of the first experiment was apparently due to large individual differences in the subjects' ability to run the 100-yard dash, regardless of the shoes. In the second experiment, we eliminated much of the variability due to individual subject differences by choosing subjects that were more alike.

How could we make the subjects even more alike in the two groups? By using the same subjects! You should be able to see why a within-subject experiment gives you a statistical advantage here: it is

Table 7–3.   Individual times to run the 100-yard dash for two groups of randomly chosen track-team members.

Subjects Wearing 7-mm Spikes	Time (in Seconds)	Subjects Wearing 13-mm Spikes	Time (in Seconds)
Art	10.6	Rob	10.9
Simon	10.3	Frank	11.1
Nick	10.3	Walt	10.9
Daryl	10.2	Gary	10.7
Ralph	10.4	Ken	10.9
Will	10.0	Bryan	10.8
Reuben	10.2	Dick	10.7
Ed	10.1	Stan	10.8
Fred	10.3	Rich	10.8
Wayne	10.4	Mark	11.2

Mean difference = .5 sec.

the ultimate way to minimize the individual differences between subjects. By using a within-subject design, both you and statistical tests are more likely to be convinced that any differences in performance found between the levels of the independent variable are real differences.*

Disadvantages of Within-Subject Experiments

Since there are so many practical and statistical advantages to using within-subject designs, why should we ever use between-subjects designs? Unfortunately, the within-subject design also carries some rather serious disadvantages. Some would go so far as to say these disadvantages make within-subject experiments next to worthless. Poulton has said: "The day should come then when no reputable psychologist will use a within-subject design, except for a special purpose, without combining it with a separate groups (between-subjects) design."[1]

The basic problem is that once subjects are exposed to one level of the independent variable, there is no way to change them back into the people they were prior to being exposed. The exposure has done something irreversible to the subject, so we can no longer treat him as a pure, uncontaminated, naive subject. How is the subject changed?

One way a subject can change is to learn. Suppose we wanted to know whether it takes someone longer to learn to type on a manual typewriter or an electric typewriter. We decide that because there are likely to be large individual differences in typing ability, we will use a within-subject design. We take ten subjects and find out how many hours they have to practice in order to type 30 words per minute on a

---

*Those among you with a bent toward statistical rigor may have shuddered and blanched at my attempt to make the logic of inferential statistics intuitively palatable. I'll be a little more rigorous in Chapter 9. But not much.

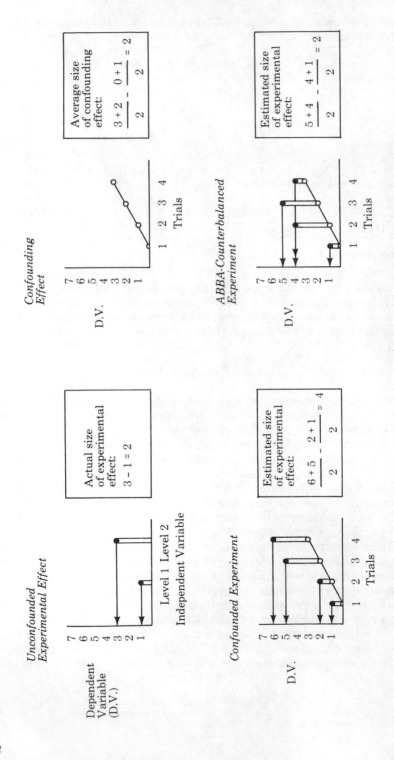

Figure 7–1. The resultant effect of adding an experimental effect to a systematic confounding effect for a confounded within-subject design and an ABBA counterbalanced design.

manual typewriter. We then switch them to an electric typewriter and find out how many hours they have to practice to type 30 words per minute on it. We find that it takes them an average of 45 hours of practice to reach criterion on the manual, compared with 2 hours on the electric. Can we conclude that the electric typewriter is that much easier to learn on? Obviously not.

During the first part of the experiment, in addition to learning the specific skill of using a manual typewriter, the subjects were also learning a general typing skill. The general skill is confounded with the specific skill. By the time the subjects typed on the electric typewriter, their general typing skill was undoubtedly at a higher level than when they started the experiment. Any time such an effect changes systematically across the trials, we must be careful to keep the effect of our independent variable from becoming confounded with it.

To illustrate how we might avoid confounding variables in this way, let's consider another experiment. Suppose you are a physical-education major who is interested in the difference in a person's ability to shoot basketball foul shots with the preferred or nonpreferred hand. To minimize the effect of prior experience, you decide to use subjects who have never shot a basketball. And to minimize the effect of individual differences in shooting ability, you decide to use a within-subject design. You choose as your dependent variable the number of shots made during a 30-second trial. Being a good experimental psychologist, you realize your experiment has a potentially confounding effect: the subjects will learn a general basketball-shooting skill as they go and will be more likely to make more shots with each additional trial regardless of which hand they are using. How can you get rid of this confounded confounding effect?

Counterbalancing

One way to minimize the effect of a systematic confounding variable like learning is to *counterbalance* the order in which you present the levels of the independent variable. One of the more frequently used techniques is called *ABBA counterbalancing*. If we call A shooting the ball with the nonpreferred hand and B shooting the ball with the preferred hand, then ABBA simply indicates the pattern in which subjects will shoot. This pattern serves to counterbalance the confounding effects across the two levels of our independent variable.

Why does ABBA counterbalancing work? Figure 7-1 illustrates a two-level experiment. The panel labeled *Unconfounded Experimental Effect* shows the actual experimental effect for an average subject. At Level 1, the subject's performance is 1 unit of our dependent variable (number of baskets), and at Level 2 it is 3 units. In the basketball example, this part of the figure illustrates that right-handed subjects who had never shot a basketball would make an average of one basket if they used their left hand (Level 1) on the first 30-second trial, or three baskets if they used their right hand (Level 2). The actual size of the experimental effect is the difference in the dependent variable at the

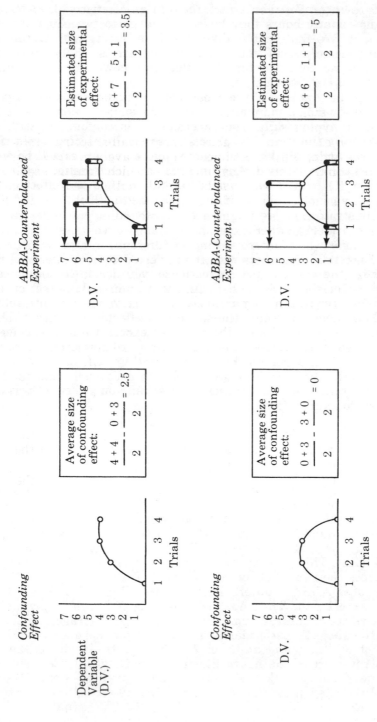

Figure 7–2. The resultant effect of adding an experimental effect to a nonlinear increasing confounding effect and to a confounding effect that first increases and then decreases. In both cases, the ABBA counterbalancing fails to eliminate the confounding effect.

two levels of the independent variable, or, in this case, 2. It is this experimental effect that we are trying to find when we carry out the experiment. However, the actual experimental results will contain effects other than the pure experimental effect, such as the effect of the confounding variable (learning). Thus, what we need to do is determine the effect of the confounding variable so that we can subtract it out of the experimental results and be left with only the experimental effect.

The panel labeled *Confounding Effect* shows a systematically increasing effect due to trials. In the basketball example, this effect could be learning, or an increase in general basketball-shooting skill. The figure indicates that the subject improves by an average of two baskets for each additional 30-second trial no matter which hand is used.

The panel labeled *Confounded Experiment* illustrates the experimental results we would expect if the experimental effect were added to the confounding effect. In this case, the subject would shoot with the left hand on the first two trials, making one and two baskets, and with the right hand on Trials 3 and 4, making five and six baskets. If we were now to estimate the size of the experimental effect from these results without taking into account the confounding effect, we would subtract the average number of baskets in the left-handed condition from the average number in the right-handed condition. However, by this process we would have overestimated the size of the effect; our estimated experimental effect of 4 is equal to the sum of the actual experimental effect and the average confounding effect. We want a way to determine the actual experimental effect alone.

Suppose we did the experiment using ABBA counterbalancing. The final panel shows the expected experimental results when Level 1 is used on Trials 1 and 4 and Level 2 on Trials 2 and 3 (ABBA). Here the estimated size of the experimental effect is the same as the actual experimental effect. The counterbalancing effectively eliminates the confounding effect without our actually having to determine what the confounding effect is and subtract it out.

While the counterbalancing scheme was successful under the conditions we had outlined in this experiment, let's see what would happen if we changed some of the conditions. For example, it is unusual for a confounding effect to form a perfectly straight line (linear) as in Figure 7-1. A typical learning curve (the most usual confounding effect) looks a lot like the upper-left panel of Figure 7-2 (nonlinear): an initial large increase in performance is followed by progressively smaller changes. If we combine the experimental effect from Figure 7-1 with this nonlinear confounding effect in an ABBA-counterbalanced experiment, we would expect to get the results shown in the upper-right panel. The counterbalancing eliminates some but not all of the confounding effect; the experimental effect is still overestimated by 1.5.

Sometimes you might have a confounding effect similar to the one shown in the lower-left panel. Imagine, for instance, that the subject's basket-shooting skill improves rapidly at first but slows up once fatigue begins to set in. By the fourth trial the subject has taken about 100 shots and is back to his or her original performance level due to fatigue. In

this case, ABBA counterbalancing makes things worse instead of better. The estimated size of the experimental effect is three times what it should be. In fact, we would have eliminated the confounding effect in this case by ordering the presentation sequence: Level 1 on Trials 1 and 2, and Level 2 on Trials 3 and 4. We have seen, then, that ABBA counterbalancing can eliminate the effects of a confounding variable in within-subject experiments, but only if the confounding effect is linear. If the effect is nonlinear, we must choose a different counterbalancing technique or else design a between-subjects experiment.

An ABBA-counterbalancing technique attempts to counterbalance sequence effects in a completely within-subject manner: the same subject gets both orders. Other counterbalancing techniques make order a between-subjects variable by counterbalancing order across subjects. In the simplest two-level case, one group of subjects would receive AB and a second group BA. If you use this method, the confounding effect does not have to be linear. However, you are still making the assumption that the effect of having B follow A is just the reverse of the effect of having A follow B. This assumption is sometimes called an assumption of *symmetrical transfer.**

Suppose you are a plant manager and you want to know whether paying your workers 10¢ for every widget they make will cause them to make more widgets than paying them 5¢ a widget. Let's say that the

---

* Sometimes it is also called *nondifferential transfer.*

workers are now paid only a base salary and nothing extra per widget. You decide to take one group of workers and on the first day pay them 5¢ per widget. On the second day you switch to a 10¢ rate. A second group gets the reverse order. What do you think the outcome would be?

Past research indicates that the first group's production will increase greatly on the first day and will increase only a little more on the second day. The second group's production on the first day will go up about the same amount but will decrease to almost the original level on the second day.

As you can see in Figure 7-3, the size of the drop in production when Group 2 goes from 10¢ to 5¢ is much greater than the increase when Group 1 goes from 5¢ to 10¢. This result is an asymmetrical-transfer effect caused by contrast. For Group 1, 5¢ looks much better

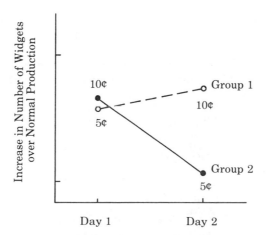

Figure 7–3. Fictitious results of an experiment that varied the amount paid to workers for producing a widget.

than nothing so they work about as hard as they can on the first day. When the rate is raised to 10¢ on the second day, they cannot work very much harder than they already are. Group 2 also jumps to nearly maximum output on the first day when they are paid at a 10¢ rate. When they take a 50% pay cut on the second day, their production falls rather rapidly. When you get such asymmetrical-transfer effects, no form of counterbalancing can save a within-subject design.

As you add more levels to your independent variable, you increase the complexity of a complete counterbalancing procedure. In a completely counterbalanced design, every level has to occur an equal number of times and also follow every other level an equal number of times. Table 7-4 shows completely counterbalanced designs for two-, three-, and four-level experiments. As you can see, complete counterbalancing can become a monumental task when you have a large number of levels or many independent variables. You can sometimes use

Table 7–4. Completely counterbalanced designs for two-, three-, and four-level independent variables. A, B, C, and D represent the levels.

| *Two Levels of Independent Variable* | |
Number	*Order of Levels*
1	AB
2	BA

| *Three Levels of Independent Variable* | |
Number	*Order of Levels*
1	ABC
2	ACB
3	BCA
4	BAC
5	CAB
6	CBA

| *Four Levels of Independent Variable* | | | |
Number	*Order of Levels*	*Number*	*Order of Levels*
1	ABCD	13	CABD
2	ABDC	14	CADB
3	ACBD	15	CBAD
4	ACDB	16	CBDA
5	ADCB	17	CDAB
6	ADBC	18	CDBA
7	BACD	19	DABC
8	BADC	20	DACB
9	BCAD	21	DBAC
10	BCDA	22	DBCA
11	BDAC	23	DCAB
12	BDCA	24	DCBA

a technique called *partial counterbalancing* in which you randomly choose only some of the orders while making sure that you still have each level occur the same number of times in each position. With large experimental designs, you can also assign levels *randomly* or *randomize within blocks* as described in Chapter 1.

You have learned that a counterbalancing technique is often necessary to minimize the sequential confounding effects found in some within-subject experiments. You should also be aware of the assumptions underlying the technique you are using (such as linear confounding effects and symmetrical transfer) and should try to use a counterbalancing technique that allows you to meet the assumptions. However, in experiments such as those having asymmetrical transfer, it may be impossible to meet the assumptions, and you will have no choice but to use a between-subjects design.

Range Effects

Suppose you are back in the widget factory ordering a new set of working tables for widget assembly. You must choose the height of the tables and you want to make sure that the tables are the right height to maximize production. You decide to do an experiment to determine the correct height. You take one group of workers, Group A, and have them sit at tables of varying heights while you count how many blocks they can turn over during a 3-minute period of time. The table heights you choose are −10, −6, −2, +2, +6, and +10 inches below or above elbow height. Having read this book, you realize that you may have a problem with sequential-ordering effects, so you carefully counterbalance the order of table heights.

After you have completed the experiment your boss suggests that she would like to see you test some tables of even lower height. You design another experiment just like the first, except this time you have Group B use tables of the following heights: −18, −14, −10, −6, −2, and +2 inches below or above elbow height.

Figure 7-4 shows the actual results of this experiment.[2] The startling thing about the results is that the best table height is quite different for the two groups. Group A performed best at about elbow height and Group B at 6 inches below elbow height. Why is this? In learning a task like turning over blocks at a table of a given height, subjects also learn a skill that is useful for other tasks, like turning over blocks on a table of a different height. The more alike the two table heights, the better the subject can transfer the skill from one height to the other. This is simply a basic principle of learning. So, if we consider the block-turning experiment to be a learning experiment, we would expect subjects to perform best at the table height that is most like all of the other table heights used in the experiment. Table 7-5 shows the average number of inches difference in height between each table height and the other five heights presented for each group. If we expect the highest rate of work for the task that is most similar to the other conditions presented in

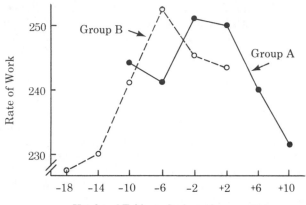

Height of Table in Inches Above or Below
Elbow

Figure 7–4. The effect of the range of table heights presented on the number of blocks turned during 3-minute trials. The range effect due to this within-subject design is seen in the superior performance at the middle heights for each group. (From "Series Effects in Motor Performance Studies," by J. E. Kennedy and J. Landesman, *Journal of Applied Psychology,* 1963, *47,* 202–205. Copyright 1963 by the American Psychological Association. Reprinted by permission.)

each experiment, we could do a fairly good job of predicting Figure 7-4 from Table 7-5. You can now see why it is called a range effect: subjects tend to have the highest level of performance in the middle of the range of levels presented since transfer of learning is highest in the middle of the range. Range effects can result from a within-subject experiment whenever stimuli or responses can be put in a consistent order. Poulton has noted examples of range effects throughout most areas of experimental psychology.[1]

Although range effects caused Poulton and others to warn against within-subject experiments, other investigators argue that in many cases within-subject experiments should be used. Greenwald, for instance, has pointed out that a range effect is simply a *context effect.* The subject comes to the experiment with a context already established. In the table example, for instance, people are already experienced at using certain table heights.[3] He suggests that repeatedly presenting a subject with only one level of the independent variable, as in a between-subjects

Table 7–5. Average number of inches difference between each table height and the other five heights presented.

| | Table Height | | | | | | | |
	−18	−14	−10	−6	−2	+2	+6	+10
Group A			12	8.5	7.2	7.2	8.5	12
Group B	12	8.5	7.2	7.2	8.5	12		

experiment, will not eliminate context. As repeated trials are given at a single level of the independent variable, a new context develops—the context of the single level. For these reasons, Greenwald claims that context effects cannot be avoided by using either type of design. He suggests that a more important question to ask in choosing a design is to what situation you plan to generalize your results.

For example, in our violent-TV experiment, it could be more artificial to repeatedly expose a child to one level of violence (a between-subjects design) than to expose the child to several different levels. Since we would like to generalize the results to a real-life situation having many levels, perhaps we should choose a within-subject design. That is, the range used in the experiment should approximate the range found in the situation to which we are generalizing. As an experimenter, then, while you should be aware that range effects could alter the outcome of your experiment, you should choose the design that allows you to generalize your results to the appropriate situation.

BETWEEN-SUBJECTS EXPERIMENTS

For the most part, we can just turn around the arguments for the advantages and disadvantages of within-subject designs to arrive at the disadvantages and advantages of between-subjects designs. There are some additional practical reasons for doing between-subjects experiments, however.

Because each subject performs under only one level of the independent variable in a between-subjects experiment, we can collect more data at that level during a single experimental session. Because subjects are likely to get tired or lose interest in what they are doing, it is easier to keep the total experimental time short for each subject. You can also avoid bringing subjects back for more than one experimental session, which is an advantage since the number of subjects who actually complete an experiment tends to decrease dramatically with each additional session required.

Matching

One way to gain the advantages of a between-subjects experiment yet avoid some of the problems of large individual differences between groups of subjects is to use a *matched-groups* design. This simply means that an attempt is made to have the same kind of subjects assigned to each level of your independent variable. In the typical between-subjects experiment, you hope that the subjects at each level are pretty much alike, and you have randomization on your side. Random assignment of subjects makes it likely that the groups will be essentially equivalent, and this becomes more likely the larger the groups. However, because this is a random process, there are times when the difference between the subjects assigned to each level, rather than your independent variable, will cause the differences in the dependent variable.

That is, your experiment may be confounded by subject differences. By matching your groups of subjects, you can minimize this possibility. On what basis can you match the groups?

You must match your groups on a variable that is highly correlated to the dependent variable. In our track-shoe experiment, it would have been a waste of time for us to match the two groups of runners on the basis of IQ scores. Fast minds are not related to fast feet. However, we could have had each subject run the 100-yard dash in tennis shoes first and then make up pairs of subjects: the two fastest, the two next fastest, and so on. We could then flip a coin to assign one member of each pair to each of the track-shoe conditions. In this way, we know that the groups are somewhat equivalent in running speed prior to introducing the independent variable. In this experiment, we are assuming a large correlation between tennis-shoe running times and track-shoe running times since the lower the correlation between the matching variable and the dependent variable, the less we gain by matching.

Through matching, we decrease the probability of being wrong when we say that the independent variable caused a change in behavior. Matching can also provide a statistical advantage in that when matched groups are used, a statistical test is more likely to say that a given difference in the scores of the dependent variable is due to the independent variable rather than to chance. That is, the tests are more sensitive to any difference associated with the independent variable.

MATCHED-GROUPS DESIGN

To illustrate this principle, Table 7-6 again lists the randomly chosen subjects who ran the dash in 7-mm spikes. The scores in parentheses are the subjects' times for running the dash in tennis shoes. We could now have a large number of additional subjects run the dash in tennis shoes and choose those that matched our original group. We then have this new group run the dash in 13-mm spiked shoes and again find that there is an average .5-second increase in running time for the 13-mm subjects. Would you be more likely to attribute the .5-second difference to the independent variable in the original random-groups experiment or in this matched-groups experiment? Statistical tests make decisions in much the same way you do.

Table 7–6. Individual times to run the 100-yard dash for two groups of matched subjects.

Subjects Wearing 7-mm Spikes		Time (in Seconds)	Subjects Wearing 13-mm Spikes		Time (in Seconds)
Mike	(12.2)	11.7	Vic	(12.2)	12.2
Homer	(12.8)	12.2	Jack	(12.8)	12.6
Randy	(13.5)	12.9	Barry	(13.5)	13.5
Gordon	(14.0)	13.2	Larry	(14.0)	13.8
John	(14.3)	13.7	Jess	(14.3)	14.2
George	(16.1)	15.4	Stuart	(16.1)	15.8
Harry	(16.7)	15.8	Harvey	(16.7)	16.2
Tim	(17.0)	16.0	Sid	(17.0)	16.6
Bob	(18.7)	18.2	Pat	(18.7)	18.7
Bill	(19.7)	19.1	Joe	(19.7)	19.6

One disadvantage in doing matched-groups experiments is that it takes longer to match the groups, so that experiments sometimes require two sessions, one for the pretest and one for the experiment itself. If you are planning to use many subjects anyway, the chances of getting large differences between groups using random assignment is quite small, and the hassle of matching might not be worth the effort.

A final consideration is that the matching process may cause some problems itself. We assumed in the example that the tennis-shoe pretest did not differentially affect the spiked-shoe test. Suppose, however, that the tennis-shoe test taught the subjects a smooth-shoe running technique that they could transfer to a later test. We might predict that the smoother the shoes on the later test the faster they will run. Since the shorter spikes are more like smooth shoes, they will cause faster times. In this case, the pretest would differentially affect the subjects' performances at the two levels of the independent variable.

Thus, matched-groups designs can be valuable under certain conditions, but they can also cause more problems than they solve. You should weigh the pros and cons of using a matched-groups design for your own experiment.

SUMMARY

There are two basic ways to assign subjects to the levels of the independent variable: you can assign different subjects to each level or assign the same subject to all levels. The former method gives you a *between-subjects experiment,* the latter a *within-subject experiment.* The practical advantages of a within-subject design include using fewer subjects and minimizing training and instruction time. There are also statistical advantages in that you can eliminate variability due to individual differences in subjects. One of the disadvantages of within-subject designs is the necessity to *counterbalance* sequence effects. An *ABBA counterbalancing* can control for sequence effects within a subject, but you must be able to assume that the sequence effect is linear. *Complete counter-balancing* of order across subjects is also possible, but you must still make an assumption of *symmetrical transfer* between conditions. In large experiments where complete counterbalancing is not possible, one can use *partial counterbalancing, random assignment,* or *randomization within blocks.* Even counterbalancing will not overcome *range effects* in experiments where the stimuli or responses may be consistently ordered.

While between-subjects experiments require more subjects and have increased variability due to individual differences in subjects, they do offer the advantage of allowing shorter experimental sessions and making counterbalancing unnecessary. Individual differences between the subjects in the groups assigned to each level of the independent variable can be reduced by using a *matched-groups procedure,* although the added effort of matching is often not worth the gain in experimental sensitivity.

REFERENCES

1. Poulton, E. C. Unwanted range effects from using within-subject experimental designs. *Psychological Bulletin,* 1973, *80,* 113–121.
2. Kennedy, J. E., & Landesman, J. Series effects in motor performance studies. *Journal of Applied Psychology,* 1963, *47,* 202–205.
3. Greenwald, A. G. Within-subjects designs: To use or not to use? *Psychological Bulletin,* 1976, *83,* 314–320.

How to Choose an Experimental Design

8

A carefully conceived and executed design is of no avail if the scientific hypothesis that originally led to the experiment is without merit.*

So far we have been pretending that all experiments have only one independent variable with no more than two levels. However, this restriction has been more for the purpose of discussion than it has been a reflection of the real world. Most of the experiments that you will want to do will use more than two levels of each independent variable and more than one independent variable. In this chapter we will discuss some of the general strategies you could use in designing progressively more complex experiments.

SINGLE-VARIABLE EXPERIMENTS

Two-Level Experiments

The simplest experiment we could choose to do would be an experiment with one independent variable having two levels. Some investigators like to call the groups exposed to these levels the experimental group and the control group. We will stick to the term *level* since it is not always obvious which condition of an independent variable should be the control condition.† In any case, we must use at least two levels to

---

*Kirk, R. E. *Experimental design: Procedures for the behavioral sciences.* Monterey, Calif.: Brooks/Cole, 1968.

† For example, if we decided to vary sex (not how much you get, but which you are) as the independent variable in an experiment, should we call males or females the control group? Feminists and masculinists could argue for days over this issue so why not avoid it altogether and assign the groups to Level 1 and Level 2?

have a real experiment. Otherwise, it would be impossible to say that a change in the independent variable caused a change in the subject's behavior.

Until the last 30 years, the typical experiment reported in the psychological literature was a single-variable, two-level experiment. Since our science was very young, investigators were more concerned with finding out whether an independent variable had any effect at all than with determining the exact nature of this effect. In addition, they had not yet developed some of the statistical tests required to analyze the more complex experimental designs; in some cases, tests existed but were generally not well known by the average investigator.

Nowadays editors frown on experimenters who submit a single two-level experiment to their journals. Psychology has advanced far enough as a science that an experiment demonstrating only that an independent variable has some effect is considered but a first hesitant step toward specifying the exact relationship between the variable and the behavior. Nevertheless, you may wish to choose a simple design for your first experiment so that you can get your feet wet without drowning.

Advantages.   Actually, two-level experiments do have several advantages over more complex designs. They offer a way of finding out whether an independent variable is worth studying. If an independent variable has no effect on a person's behavior, you obviously would be wasting your time doing a more complex experiment to determine the exact nature of the effect.

The results of a two-level experiment are also easy to interpret and analyze. The outcome is simply "Yes, the variable did have an effect; the behavior changed in this direction," or "No, the variable had no effect." To determine whether any effect is real or due to chance variation, you will usually have to do a statistical test, and tests for two-level experiments are quite easy to do. They may involve no more than counting pluses and minuses, for example. Once you know which test to use, it should take you only a few minutes of hand calculation to statistically analyze your data.

Finally, in some cases you need no more information than a two-level experiment will give you, especially in applied research. If you want to pit two pieces of industrial equipment against each other and there are only two available that can do the job, a two-level experiment gives you all the information you need. The same principle holds if you are investigating two therapeutic techniques, two educational systems, two training programs, two drugs, two sexes, or two levels of any variable when only two levels are important.

Disadvantages.   Whereas a straight line is the shortest distance between two points, it is not the only line between two points. In other words, you are at a disadvantage in a two-level experiment because it will tell you nothing about the shape of the relationship between the independent and dependent variables.

Suppose we did an experiment to find out what size of type this book should be printed in so that you would have to spend as little time as possible struggling with my periphrastic prose. Since standard typewriters produce one of two types of print, we might decide to type several paragraphs on a pica typewriter and several on an elite typewriter. We could then measure the time it takes subjects to read the paragraphs. Of course, we would pretest the paragraphs for comprehensibility, counterbalance order, and do all of the good things we have learned in this book.

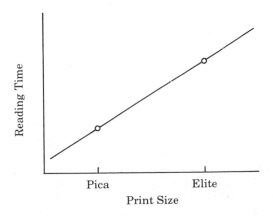

Figure 8–1. Possible results from an experiment measuring the time to read paragraphs typed in pica or elite print.

Figure 8-1 shows some fictitious results for this experiment. The arbitrary straight line drawn through the two data points indicates that the smaller the print the longer the reading time. Thus, if we wanted to decide whether we should buy pica or elite typewriters for the employees in an office typing pool, the experiment would answer our question. However, if we really wanted to know the best size of print out of all sizes and we simply chose pica and elite because they were handy, then we would not have enough information to make a decision. Our results give us no indication whether the relationship between type size and reading time is true for any print sizes other than pica and elite.

Figure 8-2 shows a number of other relationships that could also be the actual underlying relationship. You can see that not knowing the shape of the relationship makes interpolation questionable.* We cannot correctly conclude that a print size halfway between pica and elite would give a reading time halfway between those for pica and elite.

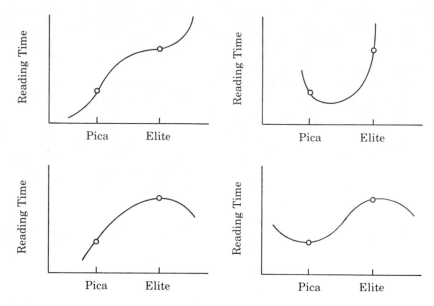

Figure 8–2. A number of possible relationships between print size and reading time. All of the functions pass through the same two data points.

Extrapolating from two points is even more dangerous than interpolating. Most psychological functions have what are called *ceiling* and *floor effects*. A ceiling effect occurs when the dependent variable reaches a level that cannot be exceeded. Typical examples of ceiling levels are: accuracy of response, 100%; probability of response, 1.0; and confidence in a response, 100%. In each case, it is physically impossible for the subject to produce a response exceeding a particular value. (You can't be more accurate than 100%, in other words.)

A floor level is a value below which the subject cannot respond. A subject cannot respond in fewer than zero seconds, for example, or give fewer responses than none. If we take our two data points and extrapo-

---

* Interpolation is an estimate of intermediate values within a known range; extrapolation is an estimate of values beyond a known range.

INTERPOLATING BETWEEN TWO
POINTS IS RISKY.

EXTRAPOLATING BEYOND TWO
POINTS IS EVEN MORE DANGEROUS!

late to values above a ceiling or below a floor we won't be in the attic or basement, we'll be in hot water! And sometimes it is not obvious where a ceiling or floor should be. In order to avoid these problems, you should make it a rule in a two-level experiment not to interpolate or extrapolate beyond the levels used in the experiment.

Two-level experiments are also of limited theoretical value. We agreed in Chapter 1 that science is built on relationships and that scientists use theories to explain the relationships found in experiments. Each theory competes with other possible theories until an experiment is done that supports one theory to the exclusion of the others. A two-level experiment will seldom help us to eliminate competing theories, since a nearly unlimited number of theories will predict that an independent variable will cause a dependent variable to change in a particular direction. Thus, while simple two-level experiments do add to our body of knowledge, typically they do little to advance scientific theories.

Multilevel Experiments

Multilevel experiments are single-variable experiments presenting three or more levels of the independent variable. They are also called *functional experiments* by some investigators, because they allow you to get some idea of the shape of the function relating the independent variable to the dependent variable.

Advantages. The major advantage of a multilevel experiment is that the results allow us to guess the nature of the experimental relationship. Even if an experiment has only three levels, it still provides us with a much better idea of the relationship than a two-level experiment does.

Suppose we wanted to know how a student's anxiety level influences his or her test scores. We decide to use two introductory psychology classes and a two-level, between-subjects design. In Class 1 the instructor spends 5 minutes prior to each major exam haranguing the students about the importance of grades for success in school. She makes it clear that students with the best grades get the best jobs, that students with college degrees earn a far larger salary, and that the university is a bit overcrowded at the moment.

In Class 2 she also gives a 5-minute talk prior to each exam. In this talk, she reminds the students that making a good grade is not as important as learning the material. She tells them that 10 years from now they won't even remember what grade they got on this test anyway. We are careful to control all of the potential confounding variables, such as class composition, test difficulty, and class instruction; thus, we decide that the difference in test scores can be attributed to the anxiety produced by the talk. Assuming that the first speech causes a high level of anxiety in the students and the second a lower level, we might get the results shown in Figure 8-3.

At this point the best guess we could make is that there is no relationship between anxiety level and average test score; a straight line drawn through the two points is flat. Suppose, however, that we had decided on a multilevel design and added a third anxiety level, a neutral level in which the instructor gives a 5-minute speech simply reminding the students of some procedural details. Figure 8-4 shows some imaginary results for this multilevel experiment.

When we graph the third data point, we see that there is, in fact, an important relationship between anxiety level and test scores,* al-

---

*If you have had a course in motivation or attention, you may recognize this function as a form of the Yerkes-Dodson law, in which an inverted "U" describes the relationship between arousal and learning. Good for you!

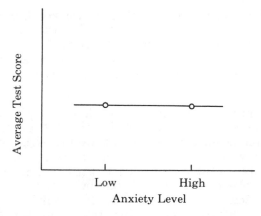

Figure 8–3. Imaginary results from a two-level experiment varying the anxiety level of students and measuring their average test score.

though there is still some doubt about the exact shape of the function. Any of the three shapes shown in Figure 8-4 would seem to be good possibilities; and, since most psychological functions do not take sharp turns or change directions rapidly, we know there aren't many other relationships possible. As you can see, the third data point allows us to get a much better idea of what the experimental relationship is, as well as to find the existence of a relationship in the first place. As we add progressively more levels to our experiment, we can make even better guesses about the true functional relationship between the independent and dependent variables. We can also interpolate and extrapolate from our data points with more confidence.

This example also illustrates a second advantage of a multilevel experiment: generally the more levels you add, the less critical becomes

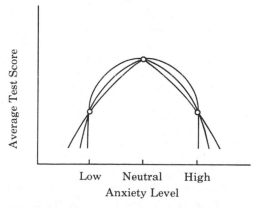

Figure 8–4. Imaginary results from a three-level experiment varying the anxiety level of students and measuring their average test score.

the range of the independent variable. As you recall from Chapter 6, we determined that, while the range should be realistic, it should also be large enough to show a relationship if one exists. Obviously it becomes easier for us to satisfy both of these requirements as more levels of the independent variable are represented in the experiment.

Disadvantages. From a practical point of view, the major disadvantage of a multilevel experiment is that it requires more time and effort than a two-level experiment. Recall that, every time we add a level to a between-subjects experiment, we increase the number of subjects needed. In within-subject experiments, additional levels do not increase the number of subjects needed, but they do increase the total time of the experiment and make counterbalancing schemes more ponderous.

The statistical tests required to analyze multilevel experiments are also a bit more difficult to do. They take more time, and it is more difficult to interpret the data in light of the statistical test.

In weighing the advantages and disadvantages of two-level versus multilevel designs, these slight additional costs of adding levels to the independent variable are usually more than offset by the value of the information gained. This benefit is especially valuable for the first few extra levels added to the design. At some point, of course, adding more levels will do little to increase our knowledge of the experimental relationship.

Baseline Experiments

Individual versus grouped data. Some investigators claim that the way the majority of psychologists do experiments is at best misleading and at worst pointless. The loudest revolutionary in this group has been Sidman, who claims that the kind of traditional experiments that you have been learning about in this chapter tell us little about an individual's behavior.[1] Sidman points out that experiments usually tell us about the behavior of some imaginary average subject who does not accurately reflect any real individual subjects. He claims that most experimenters use groups of subjects and pretend that the behavior of individual subjects in the group resembles the average behavior of the group. He argues that there are times when no subject in the group may behave anything like the average group behavior.

To illustrate this point, consider an experiment designed to find out how quickly a person can learn a simple analogy by being exposed to examples. The first item might be: *edit* is to *tide* as *recap* is to _____. The answer is *pacer,* since *pacer* is *recap* spelled backward. The next item might be: *pets* is to *step* as *tool* is to _____. Again, the answer is *tool* spelled backward, or *loot*. We give each subject 3 seconds to solve an item before presenting the next item. We expect learning to occur in an all-or-nothing fashion. That is, we assume that at some point the subject will cry "Aha!" or "Eureka!" and from then on get every item correct.

Figure 8-5 shows fictitious individual results for ten subjects; Figure 8-6 shows a group curve representing the average subject. You can

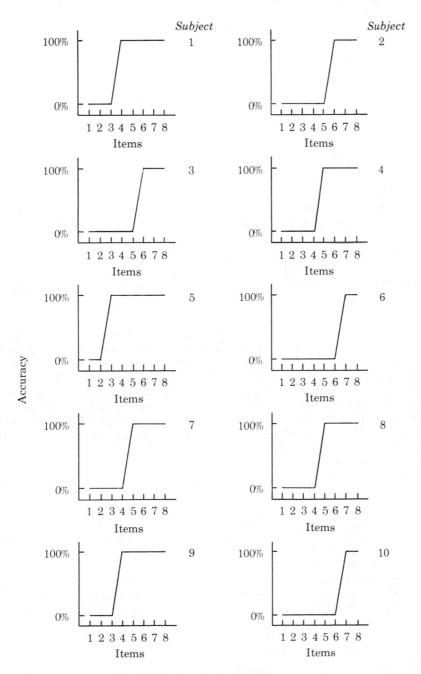

Figure 8–5. Possible individual results for ten subjects in an analogy experiment. Once subjects learn the rule for solving this type of problem, they are correct on all subsequent items.

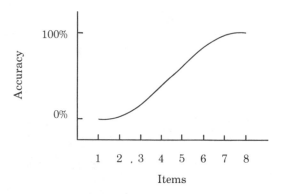

Figure 8–6. The group curve for the subjects shown in Figure 8-5. Note that the group curve is a poor representation of any individual subject.

see that the group curve in Figure 8-6 does not represent any of the individual curves in Figure 8-5. The group curve might cause us to conclude that subjects learn the solution gradually; however, every subject actually appears to have gone from solving none of the items to solving all of the items on a single trial.

Because of such discrepancies, Sidman believes that group performance seldom tells us much about how individual subjects perform. Psychologists decided to use groups in the first place because the behavior of single subjects is so variable and because an individual subject's variability is likely to be canceled out by other subjects who happen to vary in the opposite direction. Sidman, however, says that variability is not inherent in the subject but is caused by a failure of the experimenter to control all of the variables affecting that subject. Once experimenters gain adequate control of the subject's behavior, they should no longer find it necessary to use large groups of subjects, and the way for experimenters to demonstrate that they have gained this control is to do a baseline experiment.

Baseline procedures.   To illustrate a Sidmanian *baseline experiment,* let's consider an experiment designed to find out whether punishment can be used to change the behavior of a person with cerebral palsy. Suppose a therapist is working with a cerebral-palsied patient who wishes to improve his interview skills.* Cerebral-palsied individuals often have problems controlling their head movements and so tend to lose eye contact. As an attempt to increase the amount of eye contact, which is one aspect of a successful interview, the therapist decides to devise a procedure whereby the patient gets a mild electric shock each time eye contact is broken. The patient, wishing to improve his social skills, agrees to the shock procedure.

---

*I wish to thank David A. Sachs of Las Cruces, New Mexico, for this particular example. He devised the technique described, although the results I will report are fictitious.

THE FIRST STEP IS TO
ESTABLISH A STEADY STATE...

The first step in this type of experiment is to establish a *baseline*—that is, a *steady state* at which the response rate changes very little. One of the nagging problems in baseline experiments is determining how much "very little" is. The methods for determining whether the baseline has reached a steady state vary, from a statistical criterion such as "no more than 3% change in the response rate from one session to the next" to a simple visual inspection of the data for obvious fluctuations or trends. Once a baseline has been established, the experimenter begins the experimental manipulation.

In our example, the therapist might have the patient report every day for a half-hour simulated interview. During the interview, the therapist would throw a hidden switch whenever the subject's eyes were not maintaining contact. The switch would be connected to a clock so that total time of eye contact during each half-hour session could be determined. After a number of sessions, when the therapist is satisfied that a stable baseline performance has been reached (that is, a fairly consistent time of eye contact per session), he would begin the shock procedure. Whenever the patient breaks eye contact and the experimenter throws the switch, the patient gets a short electrical shock to his forearm. The experimenter then tries to determine whether the amount of eye contact changes from its baseline rate.

Figure 8-7 shows a possible result for this experiment: The therapist decided that a stable baseline had been achieved after Session 5 and began shocks on Session 6. Once the shocks were begun, the subject's eye contact increased dramatically. By Session 10, the subject's eye contact had reached a stable *transition state,* and the experimenter discontinued the shock. By Sessions 12 to 14, the subject returned to the original baseline behavior.

An experimenter must carry out each of the operations we've described in order to have a true baseline experiment: establish a stable baseline; apply the experimental manipulation and establish a stable transition state; then show reversibility by recovering the original baseline when the experimental manipulation is removed.

The logic of the method is that, once a baseline has been obtained, it would be unlikely that an uncontrolled confounding variable would suddenly begin to affect the subject's behavior on the same trial that the

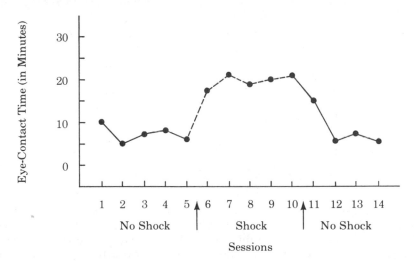

Figure 8–7. Possible results of an experiment in which eye-contact time for a cerebral-palsied patient was measured during 30-minute simulated interviews. The first five sessions provided a baseline. Shock was administered on Sessions 6–10, and baseline recovery occurred during Sessions 11–14.

experimental manipulation is made. Even if this unlikely event happened, the chances that a confounding variable would then cease to have an effect on the same trial that the experimental manipulation is discontinued would be extremely small.

To be even more convincing, an experimenter could do an *intrasubject replication,* repeating the procedure with the same subject one or more times. That is, the experimenter might again shock the subject on Session 15, continue until a stable transition state is achieved, discontinue the shock, and recover the original baseline. Each time the effect can be repeated, our confidence that the change in behavior was caused by the experimental manipulation rather than an uncontrolled confounding variable increases.

Advantages. The major advantage of a baseline experiment is that it gives us a powerful way of looking at a single subject's behavior. For instance, if the results shown in Figure 8-7 were actual data, they would go a long way toward convincing me that eye contact can be controlled by contingent shock. You would be convinced too, wouldn't you?

The results are also easy to interpret. In fact, they are so easy to interpret that baseline experimenters use no statistical tests. They say that if you need a statistical test to convince other investigators that the effect you found is a real effect and not due to chance variation, then either the effect is not strong enough to bother with, or else you need to refine your techniques to get better control over the subject's behavior (eliminate unwanted variability). A baseline procedure, then, guarantees that any effect you find will not only be real but also important.

In a traditional group experiment, if you use a large number of subjects in each group, you may find an effect that is statistically significant but is of little importance. That is, you may have chosen an independent variable that has an effect on the subject's behavior, but the effect may be small compared to other more important variables. A baseline experimental procedure, however, would not be sensitive to such unimportant effects. The variability due to the more important independent variables would blanket such real but small effects.

Another advantage of a baseline procedure is the flexibility it allows you in deciding when to impose a level of an independent variable and which level to use. Prior to doing a standard experiment, the investigator must choose the number of trials to present to each subject and which levels of the independent variable to use. Because most statistical tests require it, the investigator will then need to collect an equal number of data points for each level of the independent variable. However, investigators who use baseline designs can decide at any point in the experiment to collect more data at the present level or to change to a new level. For instance, in our example if the therapist had felt the need for more data under the shock condition, he had the flexibility to continue that condition for more sessions before attempting to recover the baseline.

He could also have decided to use an additional level of the independent variable after the experiment was underway. Suppose the change in behavior was not particularly convincing at the specific shock intensity he chose. After recovering baseline and reaching stable performance, he could then choose to try a more intense shock on the next block of trials. Thus, he is not required to use predetermined levels of the independent variable.

In addition to the advantages of easy interpretation, the elimination of statistical tests, the guarantee of finding only important effects, and flexibility, baseline experiments can also be used with only one subject. Therapists with only one cerebral-palsied patient or experimenters with individual subjects with unusual disorders, training, or talent could not use a traditional experimental design to study these single subjects. They could use a baseline procedure, however, since it is appropriate for a single subject.

Disadvantages.   Although baseline experiments offer so many advantages, most experimenters still stick to traditional experimental designs because they cannot meet the assumptions of baseline experiments. For example, the assumption that experimental effects can be reversed requires that the subject return to his or her original state at the end of the experiment. We saw in the previous chapter that there are many potential sequence and ordering effects that require counterbalancing when a within-subject design is used. A baseline experiment, of course, is a special kind of within-subject design in which effective counterbalancing is impossible. Thus, any kind of systematically changing confounding variable will prevent us from recovering the original baseline. And unless the subject's behavior returns to its former state when the experimental manipulation is removed, we do not know whether to attribute the transition-state behavior to the manipulation or to some confounding variable.

For this reason, many of the traditional areas of psychology cannot be investigated by baseline procedures. Some obviously inappropriate areas are life span, memory, and some areas of learning. Most of the changes that take place during experiments in these areas cannot be reversed ("Now forget all the words you have learned.").

SOME PROCESSES ARE
NOT REVERSIBLE.

A second disadvantage is that baseline designs do not allow us to discover small but important effects. Suppose you work for the Bell System and your job is to find out whether the time it takes a directory-assistance operator to find a number is improved by using a microfilm listing rather than a standard telephone book. As each request comes in, you record the length of the call. You have operators use the standard telephone book first until you achieve a baseline; then you have them switch to microfilm, and finally return to the book.

Figure 8-8 shows some possible results. A visual inspection of the figure would probably not convince you or me that there is any difference between using the microfilm system and using the standard telephone book. In other words, the transition state does not look any different from the baseline. However, the average call under the microfilm condition is 3 seconds faster than in the book conditions. If we had done a standard experiment, a statistical test might show such a difference to be significant. But would this be an important effect? Yes, it would be since each second saved on a directory-assistance call saves Ma Bell several million dollars. That's important!

A final disadvantage of baseline experiments is that it is difficult to determine how general any effect we find may be. Since different subjects might respond differently to experimental manipulations, our one subject may be an oddball. This criticism can be overcome, of course, by

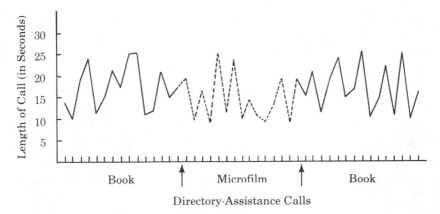

Figure 8–8. A fictitious baseline experiment measuring the length of each directory-assistance call when the operator was using a standard telephone book or a microfilm system.

redoing the experiment using additional subjects. However, the tradition in baseline experiments is to use as few subjects as possible.

Thus, it appears that baseline experimental designs can be a valuable tool for some areas of experimental psychology. When the assumptions of the design can be met, it offers a way to convincingly show the effects of important experimental manipulations. Unfortunately, the assumptions are usually so rigorous that baseline designs must be restricted to only a few areas of experimental psychology.

MULTIPLE-VARIABLE EXPERIMENTS

Most psychology experiments manipulate several independent variables at the same time. In such experiments, we have to combine the variables in an orderly way, or we won't know at the end of the experiment which variable caused the observed change in behavior.

Factorial Designs

The usual way to combine several variables is in a *factorial* combination that pairs each level of one independent variable with each level of the second and the third, and so on. The independent variables in such a design are also called *factors*.*

As an example of a factorial experiment, suppose you wanted to know whether a group with a leader would be faster at reaching a consensus opinion than would a leaderless group. You will need to decide

---

*Some investigators also call them *treatments,* which leads to the term *treatment combinations.* In building our science we emulate the Biblical folk building the Tower of Babel; no one can agree on the language. It's enough to make a new investigator a babbling idiot!

which circumstances you will control and which you will let vary: Should all of the subjects be of the same sex or not? Should communication be structured or free? Should you give the group an easy or hard problem to solve? You may find it unsatisfactory to control or randomize all of these factors. For example, you might feel that the effect of a leader on a group's efficiency might depend on the size of the group, in which case you might choose to vary both leadership and group size as factors. Suppose that you chose two levels of leadership—with and without—and four levels of size—3, 6, 10, and 20 members.

Figure 8-9 shows the usual way of representing such a factorial experiment. A *matrix* is formed with one factor on each side. The boxes within the matrix are called *cells*. Thus, the upper-left cell would represent a group with three members, one of whom would be made the leader. You can see that any row or column by itself forms a simple single-variable experiment. The example we have chosen would be called a 2 × 4* experiment since one factor has two levels and the other has four.

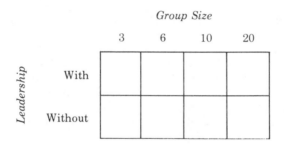

Figure 8–9. A schematic representation of a 2 × 4 factorial design. One factor, leadership, has two levels: with and without. A second factor, group size, has four levels: 3, 6, 10, and 20 members.

The number of factors represented in a factorial design is limited only by your imagination and the population of the world. Suppose we thought that group decision-making time would differ not only with leadership and size but also with the sex of the members. We make sex a third factor having three levels. Three levels? Right—male, female, and mixed (approximately half males and half females). Figure 8-10 shows a schematic of this expanded design,† which we would call a 2 × 3 × 4 factorial design.

Advantages. The major advantage of a factorial experiment is that we can study *interactions*. An interaction occurs when the relationship between one independent variable and the subject's behavior de-

---

*The "×" in this expression is read "by." In English rather than Arabic, we call this experiment a "two-by-four experiment."

† Schematically representing more than three factors becomes a bit more difficult. Four-dimensional paper is hard to come by. Experimental designs, however, are not limited by three-dimensional space. They are just hard to represent in a two-dimensional drawing.

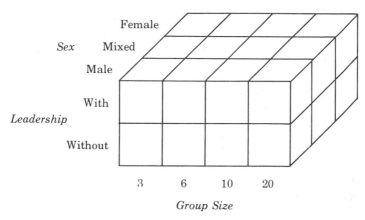

Figure 8–10. A schematic representation of a 2 × 3 × 4 factorial design. The factors are leadership (with and without), sex (male, mixed, and female), and group size (3, 6, 10, and 20 members).

pends upon the level of a second independent variable. For example, a group of three may make decisions easily with or without a leader, but as the group gets larger we may find that leaderless groups take progressively longer to reach a consensus. Thus, the relationship between leadership and decision time depends on the size of the group. Two single-variable experiments would not provide us with information about interactions; they would simply allow us to see the general effect of either leadership or group size. Only a factorial experiment will allow us to investigate the interactions.

Remember in Chapter 1 when we talked about the infinite number of circumstances that could determine behavior? We decided that, in order to do an experiment, we would have to pick one of these circumstances to be our independent variable. The other circumstances would either be controlled or allowed to vary in a random fashion. Once we determined the effect of this circumstance on behavior, we could then choose another circumstance to study. The problem with this approach is the naive assumption that, once we know the effects of each of the independent variables, we can simply add them together and account for the behavior. This assumption totally ignores interactive effects among the circumstances. The beauty of a factorial design is that the interactive effects are not ignored but evaluated.

Let's consider some of the experiments that we have used as examples and guess whether they might be influenced by interactions. Do you think that the effect of print size on reading speed would be different depending on the age of the reader? Would the effect of room temperature on typing speed depend on whether the typewriter was manual or electric? Would the effect of violent TV on children's aggressiveness be different if they watched 1 hour, 4 hours, or 8 hours of TV at a sitting? In each of these cases, our single-variable experiment could not answer the question. We would have to do a factorial experiment.

In Chapter 1 we discovered that whenever we made a circumstance into a random variable, the experimental results increased in generality but decreased in precision. On the other hand, choosing to make the circumstance into a control variable increased the precision of the outcome but decreased the generality. A factorial experiment gives us a third alternative: we can make the circumstance into another independent variable or factor, thereby increasing both the precision and generality of the result. We can generalize the outcome to a larger set of circumstances since more circumstances have been made into factors, and we know precisely what the effect is at each level of these factors. Thus, we have the best of all possible worlds, although every time we choose to make another circumstance into a factor, the experiment gets progressively more complex.

A third advantage of factorial experiments is a statistical advantage. Recall from Chapter 7 that most inferential statistical tests compare the size of any difference we find between the levels of the independent variable to an estimate of how variable the data are. We said that a difference is more likely to be declared significant by the test either if that difference is large or the variability is small. In a factorial design, when a circumstance that otherwise would add variability to the data is instead made into a factor, the amount of estimated variability in the data decreases. Thus, the more circumstances we can make into factors, the smaller the estimate of variability. The smaller this estimate, the more likely it will be that any difference we find is declared statistically significant.

Disadvantages.   With all these good things going for factorial designs, you know that they must also have some drawbacks. They do. The major disadvantage of a factorial experiment is that it is time-consuming and costly. Suppose you are again working for General Nosedive of the Air Force. You are working with a team of engineers who are designing the cockpit of a new aircraft. Since you are a psychologist and know all about humans, they expect you to tell them how to design the displays and controls and where to place them.

You are aware that some of the variables might interact with other variables so you choose a factorial design. For example, you know that the location of the airspeed indicator might affect the best altimeter location. The first factor you select is the length of the pointer on the altimeter. You find that there are four standard lengths currently in use, so you assign four levels to this factor. You also have a choice of five possible places to put the altimeter, so you select altimeter location as a second factor and assign it five levels. Your third factor is the size of the airspeed indicator with three levels. Since there are six possible locations for this instrument, you have a fourth factor. The fifth factor is the size of the joystick grip,* which has four possible diameters and five

* You nonfliers can stop snickering now. A joystick is the steering lever on an aircraft.

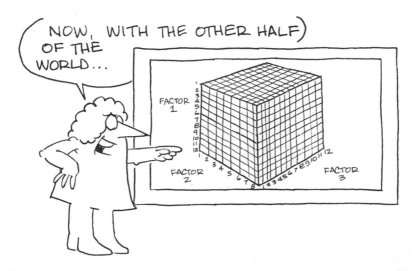

possible lengths. We have only started to consider the important variables for cockpit design, and we already have a $4 \times 5 \times 3 \times 6 \times 4 \times 5$ factorial experiment. So far the design has 7200 cells. If we assign ten subjects to each cell, we will exceed the number of pilots in the Air Force!

As you can see, whenever you add another factor to a factorial experiment, you increase the number of cells in the design by a multiple of the number of levels in that factor. At this rate, the size of factorial designs can quickly get out of hand. Since each additional cell calls for more time and effort, you must be careful not to choose an unrealistic number of factors or levels within each factor.

But we need not tell General Nosedive that it is impossible for us to give recommendations for designing the cockpit. We can use a form of *response-surface methodology* instead. This technique was developed by a chemist,[2] but psychologists now use it to make good guesses about the combined effects of many factors without having to use all possible combinations of the factors.[3]

The procedure itself is rather complicated, but an illustration should make the logic clear. Consider just two variables: altimeter size, with ten levels; and altimeter location, with eight levels. Suppose we put pilots in aircraft simulators and give them one second after a tone sounds to look at the altimeter and read the setting. We can then measure the accuracy of their readings. We might want to do a complete 10 × 8 factorial experiment, with 80 cells assigned to ten pilots each. However, we may not be able to afford an experiment with 800 subjects. The true relationship of altimeter size and location can be described by a response surface that in this case plots accuracy as a function of both altimeter size and location. Figure 8-11 shows such a response surface. In this three-dimensional plot, the most accurate combination is an altimeter of size 5 and a location at 5.

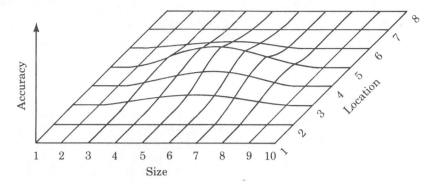

Figure 8–11. A possible response surface describing the accuracy with which subjects read altimeters as size and location are varied.

Assuming that these factors are continuous and quantitative, it is possible for us to use selected points from the response surface to estimate the complete relationship. We may select these points prior to the experiment or add them as the experiment proceeds, depending upon the methodology we use. Investigators have found that a response-surface methodology allows them to make a very good estimate of the shape of a response surface with far fewer cells than would be required for a complete factorial experiment.[3] This estimate is certainly adequate for answering the kind of question we have posed here: which combination of conditions gives the best performance?

Although the words *response surface* suggest that we must be able to plot the relationship in three-dimensional space, the methodology is mathematical in nature rather than physical and is not limited to three dimensions. A response-surface methodology would be appropriate for the six-factor cockpit experiment we discussed earlier, for example. The exact procedure for estimating a response surface is too complex to present in this book. However, we should keep in mind that the technique is available and that it helps to overcome one of the major drawbacks of factorial designs.

A second difficulty you may have with factorial experiments is interpreting the results. The statistical procedure used to analyze most factorial experiments, and all factorial experiments having more than two factors, is *analysis of variance.* This procedure requires you to make certain assumptions about the type of variability in your data. One assumption is that the variability is normally distributed in that familiar bell-shaped curve that approximates many real-world distributions. If the underlying variability in your data does not approximate a normal distribution, then an analysis-of-variance statistical test will not be appropriate.* Unfortunately, you often do not know whether you can meet this assumption until after you have completed your experiment, which

* Bradley, in his book *Distribution-Free Statistical Tests,*[4] has a good discussion of the kinds of errors you can make when you fail to satisfy this assumption.

is too bad since other statistical tests presently available for analyzing complex interactions are inadequate.[4] In such cases, you will be left with the unpleasant alternative of using a questionable statistical test or doing no statistical analysis at all. Fortunately, most factorial experiments produce distributions that are fair approximations of a normal distribution, thereby allowing you to use analysis of variance. (We will discuss analysis of variance in more detail in the next chapter.)

Even when you can satisfy the assumptions of the statistical analysis, interpreting the results of complex factorial experiments is sometimes difficult. The interactions we have mentioned so far are two-way interactions in that the relationship between one factor and the dependent variable depends on the level of a second factor. However, you could also have three-way interactions in which your two-way interaction depends on the level of a third factor. By the time you get into four-way and five-way interactions, you will no longer find it obvious how to interpret your results. We will discuss interpreting interactions in more detail in the next chapter.

We have seen that factorial experiments can offer many advantages over simple single-variable experiments. They allow you to investigate interactions, give you a statistical advantage by decreasing unwanted variability, and permit you to increase the generality of your results without decreasing the precision. However, you pay for these advantages in the time and effort expended and in the difficulty of interpreting the results. Is there a way to get some of the advantages of multiple-variable experiments without these difficulties? Yes. (Read on.)

Converging-Series Designs

Most journal articles published today report the results of a series of experiments because many experimenters choose to do a *converging series* of experiments. We will use this term to refer to any set of experiments that progressively home in on a solution, rather than tackle a problem in one fell swoop. Most series of experiments are made up of single-variable or small factorial experiments.

In one type of series, we may simply have an applied problem that is too big for a single factorial experiment, like the cockpit-design example. In this case, we might decide to do a series of smaller factorial experiments since higher-order interactions (three- or four-way interactions or larger) are of little interest. Once we find an optimal level for a particular factor in one experiment, we then make the factor into a control variable in subsequent experiments. We can then vary other important factors until we have successively manipulated all of the independent variables that might reasonably be expected to affect the subject's performance. In this way, we can progressively approach the optimal solution to our overall practical problem.

Converging operations. A more exciting form of converging-series design than those used in practical problems is one that attempts to converge on a single experimental hypothesis that will explain an observed psychological behavior. This type of experimentation has been called a *converging-operations* approach.[5] We start out the series with a number of possible hypotheses that could explain the behavior we are examining. Each experiment we do will help to eliminate one or more of our initial hypotheses until only one is left standing at the end of the series that can account for the data.

To illustrate a converging-operations technique, we can look at an experiment that investigates whether it takes longer for subjects to perceive vulgar words than nonvulgar words. Suppose the experimenter presents words to subjects using a tachistoscope, an apparatus that exposes visual material for very brief controlled periods. The experimenter presents four words, two vulgar and two nonvulgar, and instructs subjects to say the words aloud as soon as they recognize them. The experimenter finds that longer exposures are required for subjects to report the vulgar words and concludes that this finding supports the hypothesis that people unconsciously suppress the perception of vulgar material. This *perceptual-defense hypothesis* maintains that longer exposures are required to overcome this suppression.

Being an outstanding experimenter, you think of a number of other hypotheses that could explain this same finding. First, specific characteristics of the words may have made the nonvulgar words easier to read with short exposures. Second, subjects may have perceived all four words equally well but involuntarily suppressed their response on the vulgar words until they could no longer avoid it. Third, subjects may have been aware of the words and known what response to make but voluntarily withheld the response until they were positive of being correct. Thus, we have at least four possible hypotheses that can account for the results of the experiment, which are listed in Figure 8-12. We now need to do a series of experiments that will converge on one of these hypotheses and exclude the rest.

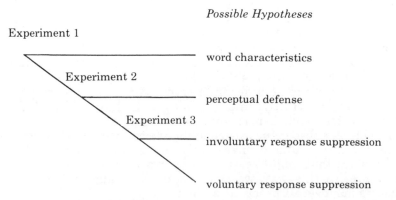

Possible Hypotheses

Experiment 1

word characteristics

Experiment 2

perceptual defense

Experiment 3

involuntary response suppression

voluntary response suppression

Figure 8–12. A schematic representation of three experiments that converge on one of four hypotheses to account for the finding that subjects require longer exposures to say a vulgar word than a nonvulgar word.

The first experiment you might do would distinguish between the word-characteristics hypothesis and the other three. You could repeat the original experiment using two different vulgar and nonvulgar words. If you again find that the vulgar words require longer exposures, then you are on your way to eliminating the word-characteristics hypothesis.* If subjects did not require longer exposure times to say the vulgar words, then our confidence in the word-characteristics hypothesis would increase.†

Assuming we eliminated the word-characteristics hypothesis, we still have to distinguish among the remaining three. In Experiment 2 we might try to determine whether subjects perceive the vulgar words at shorter exposures than they report them. We remember that a subject's galvanic skin response (GSR) gives an indication of his or her emotional response to stimuli. Thus, we decide to measure subjects' GSRs during presentation of the vulgar words in order to find out how long the words have to be exposed before they are perceived. The GSR can indicate whether subjects are perceiving a word, even though they may voluntarily or involuntarily suppress their response.

If you find that the GSR doesn't change until the exposure duration at which the subject reports the vulgar words, then the perceptual-defense hypothesis receives some support. If, however, the GSR shows that the vulgar words are being perceived at the same exposure durations as the nonvulgar words, then one of the two remaining hypotheses must be true.

To distinguish between voluntary and involuntary response suppression, you might look for an operation that would cause subjects to voluntarily change the amount of suppression. You might anticipate that when the experimenter was a member of the opposite sex from the subject, more voluntary suppression would take place than when both were the same sex. Thus, in Experiment 3, you would attempt to determine if the difference in exposure time for detecting vulgar versus nonvulgar words is less when the experimenter and subject are the same sex. If so, then the voluntary-response-suppression hypothesis is supported. If not, then involuntary response suppression seems likely.

---

* Actually a single experiment seldom eliminates a hypothesis from further consideration. For example, we may have been unlucky and selected two additional vulgar words that were still harder to read than the nonvulgar words. Or we may have failed to consider a subset of this hypothesis. For example, the effect might be due to vulgar words having a lower frequency of usage than nonvulgar words. And we recognize higher frequency words more quickly. To conclusively exclude a hypothesis, the converging operation must be completely independent of any other possible operation. By changing the specific words we have not made word frequency completely independent of word vulgarity, therefore we cannot totally eliminate this hypothesis.

† This sentence was carefully worded since we would not really have provided strong evidence supporting the word-characteristics hypothesis. In experimental psychology we design our experiments to show a difference in the dependent variable due to a manipulation of the independent variable. Showing that an independent variable caused no change in the dependent variable is very weak evidence for the proposition that it *cannot* cause a change. There are a number of other reasons for finding no change in the subjects' behavior. For example, they may have failed to follow instructions, fallen asleep, or died.

You can see how the converging operations in this example have allowed us to eliminate all but one hypothesis. The operations we used to zero in on one hypothesis were quite varied: a stimulus manipulation, a physiological measurement, and an interpersonal-relationship manipulation. We could have chosen other operations, but if the assumptions underlying our operations were correct, these other operations should converge on the same hypothesis. Every time a new operation converges on the hypothesis, we can have increased confidence in that hypothesis.

Actually, this discussion has been a bit idealized; you can seldom sit down prior to doing a converging series of experiments and detail every possible hypothesis and every operation that will be carried out to distinguish among the hypotheses. If you are like most experimenters, you will work on one experiment at a time. Only after seeing the results of one experiment will you decide on a new operation to get you closer to the true hypothesis.

As you complete more experiments in a series, you may also find that the number of hypotheses is increasing rather than decreasing. Although you can eliminate some old hypotheses, other new ones become obvious as the experimental problem is better understood. At this point it may seem that you are doing a diverging series of experiments, rather than a converging series! In fact you are still converging, but the set of potential hypotheses is simply much larger than you at first imagined it to be.

Advantages.   Most of the advantages of a converging-series approach are rather obvious from our discussion. You have a great deal more flexibility than you would have in a large factorial experiment. In a large factorial experiment, you have to decide on the factors and factor levels prior to starting the experiment, and you are then locked into this predetermined design. One bad choice can destroy a large investment of time and money. A converging series, however, gives you a number of choice points. You can choose new independent variables or levels at each of these points. You can also be much more efficient since you needn't waste time investigating factors and levels that have little effect on the dependent variable.

A converging-series design also has built-in replications. Every time you show an experimental result to be repeatable, it gains prestige in the scientific community. If you had done all three experiments in our vulgar-word example, you would have replicated or repeated the basic experimental result of vulgar words requiring longer exposures three times, providing convincing proof of the reliability of this result.

Disadvantages. There are also some minor disadvantages of converging-series designs. It is difficult and sometimes impossible to determine how variables interact if the variables are manipulated between different experiments. Under certain circumstances, you can combine two experiments from a converging series in order to analyze them as a single between-subjects factorial experiment. However, if you are really interested in interactive effects, you should do a factorial experiment.

A second disadvantage is that when comparing the results of separate experiments in the series you are always making a between-subjects comparison with all the accompanying disadvantages of between-subjects designs (see Chapter 7).

Finally, when you use a converging-series design you must analyze and interpret the results of one experiment before you can begin the next. It often takes several weeks and sometimes months to complete such an analysis. For this reason, many investigators work on more than one series at a time so that they can do an experiment from one series while analyzing an experiment from another series.

Considering the advantages and disadvantages of converging-series designs, it is easy to see why the approach has become so popular in recent years. It offers a highly efficient and flexible way to investigate both applied and basic research problems.

SUMMARY

Once you have decided on a research problem worth investigating, you must choose an experimental design. The simplest design you can choose presents only two levels of a single independent variable. This design provides a way to quickly determine if the independent variable has any effect at all on the subject's behavior. Such experiments are also easy to interpret and analyze; for some applied problems, they provide all the information necessary. However, these simple experiments can tell you nothing about the shape of the experimental relationship, so both *interpolation* and *extrapolation* are risky and the result is of limited theoretical value. Adding more levels to the independent variable will give you a better idea about the functional relationship between the independent and dependent variables. It also makes choosing a range for the independent variable less critical. A disadvantage of such *multilevel experiments* is that they require more time and effort. They are also a bit harder to interpret and analyze.

A *baseline experiment* is a special type of single-variable experiment that can show experimental effects using data from only one subject. After establishing a *steady state* rate of responding called a *baseline,* the investigator initiates the experimental manipulation until the rate of responding changes to a new *transition steady state.* The investigator then demonstrates *reversibility* by recovering the original baseline. An advantage of baseline designs is that they offer a convincing way to show important changes in a single subject's behavior. The experimenter can also be flexible in choosing when to manipulate the independent variable, and which level to change it to. These results are also easy to interpret. However, some assumptions of baseline experiments, such as reversibility, cannot be met in many areas of psychology. It is also sometimes difficult to show small but important effects and risky to generalize the findings to other subjects.

In a *factorial design,* multiple independent variables, sometimes called *factors,* are combined so that the levels of each variable occur in combination with the levels of every other variable. These designs allow you to investigate *interactions.* Every time you add a factor, the generality and precision of the results increase, while the statistical variability decreases. However, complex factorial experiments can be time-consuming and costly. The design can become so large that a *response-surface methodology* is necessary to estimate the experimental effects. Interpreting the results can also be a problem, particularly when the statistical assumptions of *analysis of variance* cannot be met.

You can use a *converging-series design* in place of a complex factorial design. This design allows you to discover *converging operations,* which progressively eliminate hypotheses until only one remaining hypothesis can account for the data. Converging-series designs offer the advantage of flexibility and also provide built-in replications. However, it is difficult to evaluate interactions between factors varying across experiments. You must also manipulate these factors in a between-subjects manner, and you must analyze one experiment before beginning the next.

REFERENCES

1. Sidman, M. *Tactics of scientific research.* New York: Basic Books, 1960.
2. Box, G. E. P., & Hunter, J. S. Multifactor experimental designs for exploring response surfaces. *Annals of Mathematical Statistics, 1957, 28,* 195–241.
3. Clark, C., & Williges, R. C. Response surface methodology central-composite design modifications for human performance research. *Human Factors, 1973, 15,* 295–310.
4. Bradley, J. V. *Distribution-free statistical tests.* Englewood Cliffs, N. J.: Prentice-Hall, 1968.
5. Garner, W. R., Hake, H. W., & Eriksen, C. W. Operationism and the concept of perception. *Psychological Review, 1956, 63,* 149–159.

How to Interpret 9
Experimental Results

> If you can't prove what you want to prove, dem-
> onstrate something else and pretend that they are
> the same thing. In the daze that follows the colli-
> sion of statistics with the human mind, hardly
> anybody will notice the difference.*

You should now be ready to collect some data. At this point, make sure
that you have made a note of all the information you will need when
reporting the experiment, such as the exact levels of your independent
and control variables and the way you counterbalanced other variables.
You may think that you will easily recall all of these facts after the
experiment is finished, but you will be amazed at how quickly these
facts merge into one undifferentiated lump. This lump usually locates
itself in your throat about the time you want to write an experimental
report. Never trust the details of an experiment to memory. If they're
important, write them down.

You will need *response sheets* to record each subject's data. At the
top of each sheet you should have a place to write such information as a
subject number, the subject's sex, the condition being presented, and any
specific comments you might wish to note about the subject or experimental session. Under this information should be lines on which to
write each subject's response values for each trial in order. If it has been
necessary to counterbalance or randomize the order of some variables,
you will later need to transfer the data to a *data sheet,* on which they
can be arranged according to independent variables and levels.

Once you have the data on paper, you are still a long way from
answering the experimental question: what effect did the independent
variable have on the dependent variable? In order to answer this question, you will need to know about several approaches to analyzing data
and how to use them.

---

*Huff, D. *How to lie with statistics.* New York: Norton, 1954.

PLOTTING FREQUENCY DISTRIBUTIONS

Suppose you are interested in the difference between women who support the feminist movement and those who do not. In particular, you want to know whether these two groups of women differ in anxiety level. You decide to ask a number of women "Do you support the feminist movement?" Those who say "yes" will be assigned to the feminist group and those who say "no" to the nonfeminist group. After assigning ten women to each group, you give them a test that has been found to reliably indicate a person's overall anxiety level. The test scores for the two groups are your raw data.*

Table 9-1 shows some fictitious scores between 0 and 100. The larger the score, the more anxious the subject. Is there a difference between groups? Looking at individual scores in this case is like listening to individual notes from a song; it's hard to tell what the melody is. We need some way to rearrange the raw data so that we can interpret them more easily. We can draw a *frequency distribution,* which is simply a plot of how frequently each score appears in the data. You may notice, however, that no score occurred more than one time. Thus, in order to make the distribution meaningful, we will need to put the individual scores into categories. We want several data points in each of the more frequently occurring categories, so we make each category include ten scores (for example, 10–19). Figure 9-1 shows such a frequency distribution for each of our two groups. The vertical axis labeled *Frequency* is simply the number of raw data points that fall into each score category.

Table 9–1. Fictitious anxiety scores for ten women who say that they support the feminist movement and ten who say that they do not.

	Feminist		Nonfeminist
Subject	*Score*	*Subject*	*Score*
1	62	11	55
2	56	12	42
3	67	13	61
4	91	14	58
5	53	15	70
6	87	16	47
7	51	17	62
8	63	18	36
9	46	19	74
10	71	20	51

Plotting a frequency distribution can be a useful first step in finding out whether there is a difference between conditions. Sometimes the experimental effect is strong enough that a visual inspection of the

---

* You will note that this experiment is really a correlational observation since we are comparing two dependent variables, the behavior of saying "yes" or "no" to the question and the test score. It is also necessarily a between-subjects manipulation since the same women cannot answer both "yes" and "no" to the question or score both high and low on the test.

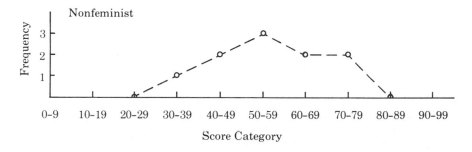

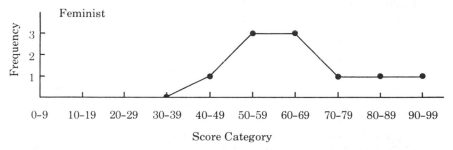

Figure 9–1. Frequency distributions for the feminist and nonfeminist anxiety scores listed in Table 9-1.

distributions will convince you that there is a difference. In this example, however, the distributions look very much alike.

Statisticians have given names to different types of distributions so that investigators can talk to each other in some common terms without having to show each other a plot of the entire distribution. We have already mentioned the properties of a *normal* distribution shown in the upper-left panel of Figure 9-2. To be normal, a distribution has to fit a complex mathematical formula. For our purposes, however, we can simply say that a distribution approximates a normal distribution if it looks

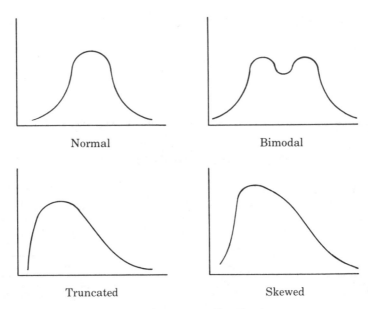

Figure 9–2.   Four types of frequency distributions.

something like the bell-shaped distribution shown in the figure. It is important to know whether your distributions are similar to a normal distribution because many of the statistical tests you will wish to use require that the data be approximately normal.

Some other types of distributions are also illustrated in Figure 9-2. In a *bimodal* distribution there are two most frequent categories rather than one. The distribution of heights for a group composed of an equal number of men and women would often be bimodal. A distribution is *skewed* if it is asymmetrical through having more scores in one of the tails. A distribution of IQ scores for Ph.D.s would be skewed since there would generally be few with low IQs. However, if a distribution looks like one of the tails has been completely chopped off, it is said to be

A TRUNCATED DISTRIBUTION

truncated. A plot of reaction times would form a truncated distribution since there is a limit to the speed with which a person can respond.*

Plotting a frequency distribution allows you to describe your data in a more orderly way than simply listing it in raw form, but it is still a rather cumbersome way to represent the results of an experiment. It would be nice to have a single number that represents how the subjects in each group performed. What we need is a way of calculating a descriptive statistic that will describe the data in this manner.

STATISTICS FOR DESCRIBING DISTRIBUTIONS

Psychologists use basically two kinds of statistics: descriptive statistics and inferential statistics. A *descriptive statistic* is simply a number that allows the experimenter to describe some characteristics of the data rather than having to report every data point. Inferential statistics will be discussed later in the chapter.

Central Tendency

One important descriptor of data is the location of the middle of a distribution. Psychologists call such a statistic an indication of *central tendency;* you probably call it an average. One way of comparing the two groups in our example would be to calculate the average anxiety score for the feminists versus the nonfeminists.

There are three common ways to express an average. The *mode* is the easiest average to calculate, but it ignores lots of data. The mode is simply the most frequently occurring score. In our example, there is no mode since no score occurred more than once. If one score had occurred twice in one of the distributions, it would have become the mode. The other numbers in the distribution could then take on any value, and as long as no two scores took on the same value, the mode would remain unchanged. Thus, since the mode uses only one property of the data to describe the average behavior (frequency), you are throwing out lots of

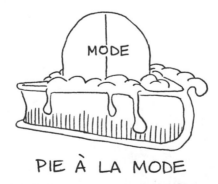

PIE À LA MODE

---

*Remember ceiling and floor effects? They usually cause truncated distributions.

information, such as the ordering and size of each number. With small samples, relying on a mode to describe your data can be risky.

The *median* is literally a middle score in that it has an equal number of scores above it and below it. To calculate a median, list all of the scores in order and then pick the middle score. If you have an even number of scores, the median falls halfway between the two middle scores. For example, in ordering the feminist scores, we find that the fifth score is 62 and the sixth is 63, so the median is 62.5. The median for the nonfeminist group is 56.5. The median does not reflect the size of the differences between scores since it uses only order as its defining principle. Thus, we can change any score in the distribution without changing the median, as long as the position of the middle score in the list remains the same. Again, we lose some information when we describe our data in terms of a median.

The *mean* is a weighted average of the scores—that is, it is the sum of all individual scores divided by the number of scores that were added. For example, to find the mean for the feminist group, we add the 10 scores for a sum of 647 and then divide by 10, with the result of 64.7 for the mean. The mean for the nonfeminist group is 55.6. The mean is the center of gravity for the distribution. Thus, since it is an average that is affected by the size of the scores, it changes whenever any score in the distribution changes.

Which average best describes a distribution? Like all interesting questions the answer is "It all depends." First, it depends on the shape of the distribution. If you have a normal distribution or any other unimodal symmetrical distribution, all three averages give you the same number. However, as a distribution becomes more skewed, the three averages get progressively farther apart. Figure 9-3 shows that the mean is most influenced by the size of the extreme scores in the right tail of the distribution. The median is influenced only because there are more scores to the right, while the mode is unaffected by these extreme scores.

You must use your judgment in deciding which measure to use. If you plot the incomes for a large group of people, you would probably get

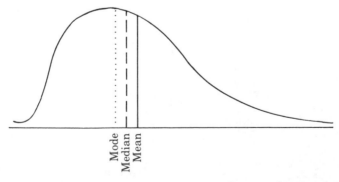

Figure 9–3. The location of the mode, median, and mean for a skewed distribution.

a distribution similar to the one in the figure. In this case a median would probably be the best average since it would be influenced less than the mean by the few folks who make outlandish salaries. You can probably think of other more extreme examples in which a few very large or very small scores can distort the mean. Whenever you must choose a measure to describe an average, you will simply have to examine the shape of the distribution, determine for what purpose the average will be used, and then use your judgment.*

Dispersion

While an average tells you something useful about a distribution, it describes only one special aspect of a distribution. A second statistic that helps describe a distribution is a measure of *dispersion,* or how spread out the scores are.

One measure of dispersion is the *range,* which we can calculate by subtracting the smallest score from the largest score. In our example for the feminist group, the range is $91 - 46 = 45$; for the nonfeminist group, the range is $74 - 36 = 38$. While the range gives some indication of dispersion, since it is determined by only the smallest and largest scores, it is totally insensitive to scores in between. For this reason, a different measure of dispersion may be more useful.

As an alternative, we could subtract the mean from each score so that we have a number indicating the deviation of each score from the mean. To get a mean deviation, we could then add up these deviations and divide by the number of deviations. However, adding the deviations gives a sum of zero, which doesn't help us much, so instead we square† each deviation (this gets rid of the plus or minus sign), add the squares, and then divide by the number of squared deviations that were added. We then have a measure of dispersion called the *variance.* A more useful measure is the square root‡ of the variance, a number called the *standard deviation.*

You may find it helpful to view the standard deviation as a way of expressing the extent of error you are making by using the mean to represent the scores in a distribution. In reality, the mean is simply the best guess you could make about any individual score; thus, the standard deviation indicates, on the average, how good a guess you have made. If all the scores were the same, the standard deviation would be zero, indicating that the mean would never be in error. As the differences among scores get larger, the standard deviation increases, as does the error you make by guessing the mean.

---

* I am assuming that you have read Chapter 5 and are trying to be fair with science. Huff's book *How to Lie with Statistics*[1] gives many humorous examples of how to make descriptive statistics like the mean into distorting statistics.

† Multiply it times itself.

‡ A number that, when multiplied times itself, gives us the variance.

PLOTTING RELATIONSHIPS BETWEEN VARIABLES

The reason you do an experiment in the first place is to find out if there is a relationship between the independent and dependent variables. While plotting frequency distributions is a good first step in analyzing your data, you will often find it useful to draw a graph to represent the experimental relationship. Graphs are not new to you. They have been cropping up from time to time in earlier chapters. To be complete, however, let's start by discussing basic concepts.

Drawing Graphs

A graph has two axes. The vertical axis (*y* axis) is called the *ordinate* and the horizontal axis (*x* axis) the *abscissa*.* When plotting experimental results, you plot the dependent variable on the ordinate and the independent variable on the abscissa. When the levels of the independent

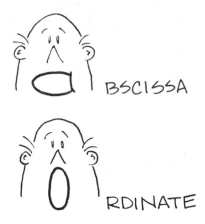

variable cannot be represented by numbers, it is usually appropriate to use a *bar graph* to represent the data. Figure 9-4 shows a bar graph for the mean anxiety scores of the feminist and nonfeminist groups.

If the independent variable is continuous, then you can draw a *histogram* as shown in Figure 9-5. A histogram eliminates spaces between the bars of a bar graph. Figure 9-5 shows some fictitious data relating the length of time patients are in therapy to their rating of self-image. Time in therapy is a continuous variable since we could choose levels anywhere on the continuum of time. In many cases it is simpler to connect the center of each bar as shown in Figure 9-5 and eliminate the bars altogether.

---

* You may find it helpful to remember which term refers to which axis by noticing the shape your mouth takes when saying the first part of each word; "ab___" is said with a horizontal mouth, "or ___" with a vertical mouth. That's the way I remember them!

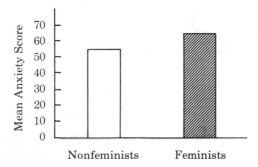

Figure 9–4. A bar graph showing the mean anxiety scores for the non-feminist and feminist groups listed in Table 9-1.

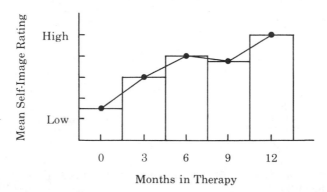

Figure 9–5. A histogram illustrating the results of a multilevel experiment relating a subject's perceived self-image to months spent in therapy (fictitious data).

Describing Functions

Several types of graphed functions are illustrated in Figure 9-6. If changing the independent variable by one unit always causes the dependent variable to change in a given direction by a constant amount, then the function is *linear;* any other relationship is *curvilinear.* When increasing the independent variable causes an increase in the dependent variable, the relationship is said to be *positive;* if it causes a decrease, it is *negative.* A function that never reverses direction (that is, portions of the function are either all positive or all negative) is a *monotonic* function; otherwise, the function is termed *nonmonotonic.* If changes in the dependent variable get increasingly larger as the independent variable increases, the function is *positively accelerated;* if the changes get smaller, it is *negatively accelerated.* A negatively accelerated function will eventually approach a particular level and appear to flatten out. The curve is actually getting closer and closer to a straight line called an *asymptote,* although the curve and asymptote never touch. Such a function is said to be *asymptotic* or to approach an asymptote.

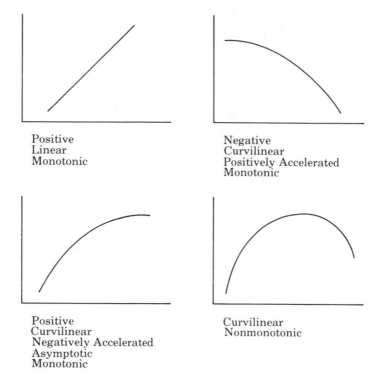

Positive
Linear
Monotonic

Negative
Curvilinear
Positively Accelerated
Monotonic

Positive
Curvilinear
Negatively Accelerated
Asymptotic
Monotonic

Curvilinear
Nonmonotonic

Figure 9–6. Graphs illustrating some terms used to describe functional relationships.

If you are coming across these terms for the first time, you may be getting a bit confused. However, as you use them to describe psychological relationships, you will find that they become more familiar and allow you to discuss your results more efficiently.

DESCRIBING THE STRENGTH OF A RELATIONSHIP

The functions in the previous section either were idealized or were plots of a descriptive statistic rather than individual data points. Rarely will you find every data point falling exactly on a smooth function, however. If we use raw data to plot an experimental relationship, we would most likely find some variability or spread around the functions. Such a plot is called a *scatterplot*.

Scatterplots

Figure 9-7 shows some examples of scatterplots. These plots could result from an experiment, in which case we would plot the relationship between independent and dependent variables, or from a correlational observation (see Chapter 1), in which case you would plot dependent variables on both axes. If you observe the spread of the points in a scatterplot, you can get some idea of how strong the relationship is. However, visual observation is a rather crude way of estimating this strength. Fortunately, when the relationship is linear,* there is a descriptive statistic that can be used for this purpose: a *correlation coefficient*.

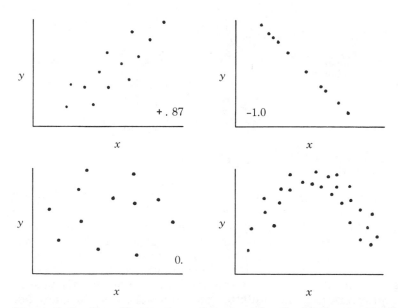

Figure 9–7. Four illustrations of scatterplots. Correlation coefficients are shown for three panels. No coefficient is given for the lower right panel because the relationship is curvilinear and a correlation ratio should be used.

Correlation Coefficients

A correlation coefficient is a number between $+1.0$ and -1.0, with the sign indicating whether the relationship is positive or negative and the size of the number indicating the strength of the relationship. A correlation of 1.0 ($+$ or $-$) indicates a perfect relationship, and 0 indicates no relationship.

Figure 9-7 shows the correlation coefficients for three sets of data. No coefficient is shown for the lower-right panel since the function is obviously curvilinear and simple linear correlation is not appropriate. (There is, however, a way of describing a curvilinear correlation called a *correlation ratio*.[2]) You can find out how to calculate a correlation coefficient by looking in any statistics text.†

---

* Actually one form of correlation uses data that can only be ranked or ordered, in which case the term *linear* is meaningless. Such a correlation can be used for any monotonic relationship.

† Several statistics texts are listed at the end of the chapter.

A STRONG RELATIONSHIP

INTERPRETING RESULTS FROM FACTORIAL EXPERIMENTS

The results of factorial experiments are more difficult to interpret than other types of experiments since they use more than one independent variable and require that we evaluate interactions. Figure 9-8 shows some fictitious results of our earlier experiment in which we measured the time it took subjects to read paragraphs typed in pica or elite print. In this case, however, we will assume that we used 8-year-old subjects in one group and 12-year-olds in another. Notice that one independent variable (print size) has been plotted on the abscissa, while the other (age) is represented by a point and line code. We can no longer just ask whether there is an effect of the independent variable on the dependent variable. We must ask three more specific questions: (1) Is there an effect of print size? (2) Is there an effect of age? (3) Does the effect of one variable depend upon the level of the other? The first two questions refer to *main effects* and the third to an *interaction*.

Main Effects

To evaluate the main effect of an independent variable we must average across the levels of the other variable. Thus, to determine the effect of print size, we need to find a point halfway between the two levels of age at each level of print size. On the first small graph in Figure 9-8, these points are indicated by an *X*. You can see that a change from elite to pica print caused a decrease in the dependent variable (time). In the second small graph, an *X* has been drawn for each age by averaging across print sizes. The dependent variable also decreases with increased age.

Interactions

To determine whether the independent variables interact, we can ask whether the effect of print size is different for each age, or, alternatively, whether the effect of age is different for each print size. The answer to

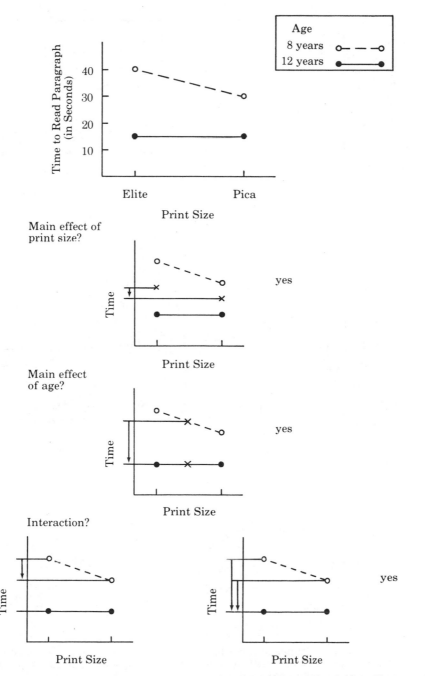

Figure 9–8. Analyzing a 2 × 2 factorial experiment for main effects and interactions.

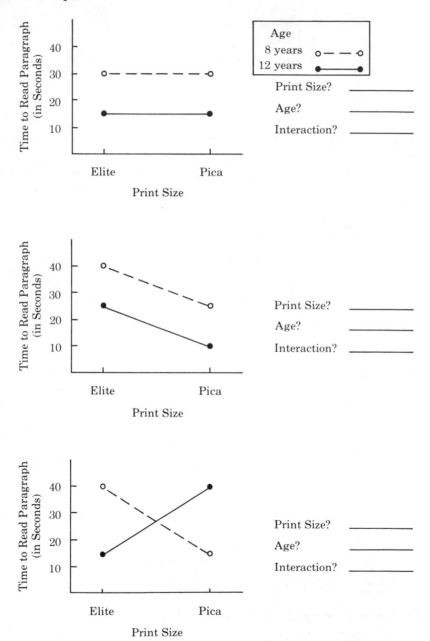

Figure 9–9.   Graphs of three possible outcomes for a 2 × 2 factorial experiment. Answer the three questions for each graph. (The answers can be
found at the end of the chapter.)

the first question is that going from elite to pica causes a decrease in reading time for 8-year-old children but no difference for 12-year-olds. The answer to the second question is that the difference between reading times for the two ages is larger for elite print than for pica. These effects are illustrated in the two bottom graphs of Figure 9-8.

Figure 9-9 shows other possible results for this experiment. Using the same procedure we have been discussing, answer the three questions for each graph.

This discussion has been limited to the simplest type of factorial experiment. When each factor has more than two levels, and when more than two factors are used, interpreting interactions becomes even more difficult, although the basic procedures for interpreting your results remain the same.

INFERENTIAL STATISTICS

I promised you at the beginning of the book that it would not be a statistics text. Thus, to find out how to calculate inferential statistical tests you will have to look in one of the books listed at the end of this chapter. Nevertheless, we should at least discuss the general logic of inferential statistics.

Let's go back to the anxiety test scores for the ten feminist and ten nonfeminist women. In order to find out whether the two groups differed in anxiety level, we plotted frequency distributions and calculated means for each group. We found that the mean for the feminist group was 64.7 and for the nonfeminist group was 55.6. Is this a real difference? Of course it is, you say: how can a difference not be a difference? And for these two samples you are absolutely correct: any difference between samples is a real difference between samples. However, what a psychologist means by the question is not "Is there a real difference between the scores for the two samples that you happened to choose for this experiment?" but rather "Is it likely that there is a difference in anxiety level between the population of feminist women and the population of nonfeminist women who could have potentially been sampled?" The goal of the experiment is to say something about the two populations that could have been chosen, not the particular samples that were.

Pretend that you are a bean farmer. You are not doing very well as a bean farmer because of bean blight. Bean blight is a mysterious bean disease that causes many beans to wither and shrivel. To find out whether you can get rid of bean blight, you plant a field with a new type of bean that may resist bean blight. After harvesting a blighted field and the new field, you have two bean bins each containing 10 tons of beans. You want to know if both bean bins are blighted.* You obviously do not wish to examine every bean in the two bins, so you decide to take a sample of 100 beans from each bin. You find 12 withered beans in the sample from the bin you know to contain blighted beans and 7 in the

* Say that quickly three times!

other sample. Obviously there is a difference between the samples, but you want to know whether there is a difference between the entire populations of the two bins. An inferential statistical test can help you answer this question. The "infer" in "inferential" comes from the fact that the test helps you infer whether there is a difference between the populations.

You, as a psychologist, face the same problem that you would face as a bean farmer. You have chosen a randomly selected sample of data from two potentially different populations (the levels of the independent variable), and you want to know whether the populations are different.

Parametric versus Nonparametric Tests

There are many inferential tests to help you make this decision. The one you choose will depend upon your experimental design and what test assumptions your data can meet. The most frequently used tests are called *parametric* tests. These tests assume that if frequency distributions were plotted for the populations of interest, they would be normal distributions. When this assumption cannot be met, you must use one of the *nonparametric* tests.

Inferential tests use different procedures for making inferences about populations. However, all tests that infer whether populations are the same provide a probabilistic statement about the likelihood that two or more samples could have come from the same population. In other words, such tests determine the probability that the observed difference among your data samples is due simply to chance variation. Any time that you randomly choose samples from the same population, it is possible, even though unlikely, to get a large difference. How unlikely must a difference be before you can conclude that the samples come from different populations?

Levels of Significance

Although it is probably unfortunate that we adhere to such a strict standard, most psychologists agree that for a result to be significant the likelihood of obtaining the observed difference in samples due to chance should be less than 1 in 20. Thus, if the samples really came from the same population distribution, you would expect to get a significant difference in only 1 out of 20 (or 5 out of 100) experiments. Some psychologists are even more careful to avoid saying that there is a difference in populations when there isn't. They will not accept a difference as a real difference unless the test indicates that it could be due to chance only 1 time in 100. These strategies are called testing at the *.05 level of significance* or at the *.01 level of significance*. When these probabilities are reached or exceeded, the result is said to be *statistically significant*.

Inferential tests are obviously an important tool for evaluating the results of psychology experiments. In fact, the development of sophisticated statistical tests has been a major influence in making psychology into a respectable science. However, we must realize the limitations of the inferential tests we use.

Misinterpreting Statistical Tests

Some experimenters believe that when a statistical test fails to show a significant difference in the levels of the independent variable, it has therefore shown that they are significantly the same. To avoid this error, we should keep in mind that inferential tests are designed to say something about the probability of getting a difference if the samples come from the same population; they tell us nothing about getting a sameness if the samples come from different populations. Consequently, negative results (ones that are not statistically significant) are seldom published in psychology journals. Our statistical tests are just not designed to tell us the probability that two samples would be this equivalent if they came from different populations; rather they tell us how probable it is that samples could come from the same population.

A second mistake some investigators make when using inferential tests is to act like the .05 and .01 levels are chiseled in stone; they wouldn't be caught dead paying any attention to a .06 level. A more realistic approach to significance levels is to treat them for what they are—a way to help you make a decision. Whenever you make a decision in the face of uncertainty, you have to consider not only the probability

of being right or wrong, but also the values and costs of being right and wrong. In other decisions you do not ignore these factors. For example, if you wanted to decide whether to fly an airplane, you would probably require a higher probability of fair weather than you would if you were simply deciding whether to carry an umbrella. The values and costs are far different. The .05 and .01 levels ignore such values and costs. Thus, you should consider the consequences of being right and wrong when you interpret the results of your experiments and not blindly test at the .05 level.

A third error you should avoid is confusing statistical significance with practical significance. Remember the fine old saying that a difference is a difference only if it makes a difference. Suppose you are an employer, and the owners of the Fast Finger Speed Reading School are trying to convince you that you should pay them to teach all of your employees how to speed read. They say that they have experimental evidence showing that people read significantly faster after taking their course. Being a skeptic, you ask how much faster. They admit that the study shows that their students read an average of ½ word per minute faster, but they insist that this difference is statistically significant. They could well be correct. By using enough subjects and collecting enough data, even tiny differences between populations can be shown to be statistically significant. As an employer, though, you care more about practical significance than statistical significance. As a scientist, you should too.

In the end, evaluating practical significance is a matter of judgment. The tools we have been discussing in this chapter should help you determine when a result is important, but the tools themselves do not establish the importance of the result. You, the experimenter, must do this by using logical arguments to convince other researchers that your differences make a difference.

SUMMARY

Once you complete an experiment, you must interpret the data listed on the subjects' response sheets. A useful first step is to plot a *frequency distribution* illustrating the number of data points occurring within categories of the dependent variable. Sometimes these distributions are similar to a symmetrical bell-shaped distribution called a *normal distribution*. Others are *bimodal* with two most frequent categories, or are *skewed* by having more scores in one tail of the distribution, or are *truncated* by having one tail of the distribution missing. There are three commonly used statistics for describing the central tendency or average of a distribution. The *mode* is the most frequently occurring category, the *median* is the middle score, and the *mean* is the center of gravity for the distribution. Two statistics are commonly used to describe the *dispersion* of a distribution: the *range* is the difference between the highest and lowest scores, and the *standard deviation* and sometimes the *variance* describe the dispersion of distributions that are approximately normal.

Graphs illustrate the relationship between the independent and dependent variables. The levels of the independent variable are put on the horizontal axis, the *abscissa*, while the values of the dependent variable are put on the vertical axis, the *ordinate*. A *bar graph* can be used to illustrate data points that represent qualitatively different categories. Either a *histogram* or points connected by lines can be used to illustrate continuous variables. In describing functions, you can indicate whether they are *linear* or *curvilinear, positive* or *negative, monotonic* or *non-monotonic, positively accelerated* or *negatively accelerated,* and whether they are *asymptotic.* The strength of an experimental relationship can be illustrated in a *scatterplot,* or, if the relationship is linear, you can calculate a *correlation coefficient.*

To interpret the results of a factorial experiment, you must determine whether there is an effect of one factor on the dependent variable at an average value of the other factors. In addition to determining this *main effect,* you must also determine whether the effect of one variable is different depending upon the levels of the other variables. Such differences are called *interactions.*

Inferential statistics are used to infer how likely it is that the difference between data samples is due to chance selection rather than due to a real difference in populations (levels of the independent variable). For an effect to be declared *statistically significant,* the probability that the difference is due to chance usually must exceed *.05* or *.01. Parametric tests* assume that population distributions are normal; *nonparametric* tests do not. Researchers sometimes misuse statistical tests by equating nonsignificant results with equivalence of conditions, by overemphasizing the .05 and .01 levels of significance, or by confusing statistical significance with practical significance.

Answers to the questions in Figure 9-9:

Top graph:	Print size?	no
	Age?	yes
	Interaction?	no
Middle graph:	Print size?	yes
	Age?	yes
	Interaction?	no
Bottom graph:	Print size?	no
	Age?	no
	Interaction?	yes

REFERENCES

1. Huff, D. *How to lie with statistics.* New York: Norton, 1954.
2. Kirk, R. E. *Experimental design: Procedures for the behavioral sciences.* Monterey, Calif.: Brooks/Cole, 1968.

SUGGESTED STATISTICS BOOKS

For the Beginning Student

Dinham, S. M. *Exploring statistics: An introduction for education and psychology.* Monterey, Calif.: Brooks/Cole, 1976.

Linton, M., & Gallo, P. S., Jr. *The practical statistician: Simplified handbook of statistics.* Monterey, Calif.: Brooks/Cole, 1975.

Spatz, C., & Johnston, J. O. *Basic statistics: Tales of distributions.* Monterey, Calif.: Brooks/Cole, 1976.

For the Advanced Student

Bradley, J. V. *Distribution-free statistical tests.* Englewood Cliffs, N.J.: Prentice-Hall, 1968.

Hays, W. L. *Statistics for the social sciences* (2nd ed.). New York: Holt, Rinehart and Winston, 1973.

Kirk, R. E. *Experimental design: Procedures for the behavioral sciences.* Monterey, Calif.: Brooks/Cole, 1968.

How to Report Experimental Results

10

A psychologist's research is complete when the results are shared with the scientific community.*

The (scientific) writer quite properly reacts to the pressure toward conformity with the writing practices of his group, but he errs if he succumbs abjectly. He needs to qualify and to define exactly, but the danger is that his sentences can become so impossibly larded with subordinate phrases and clauses that even his close associates cannot read them.†

We are all blind seekers after truth
Confused by the noisy rabble of words
Whether we shall ever say what we mean
Or mean what we say
We know not,
And only our doing
Will teach us in its hour.‡

There was a classic philosophical debate a few decades back that went something like this: if a tree falls in the forest and nobody is there to hear it, did it make a sound? The debate was whether a person had to hear a sound for the sound to be a sound. What do you think? In reporting research, we can ask a similar question: is research research if nobody hears about it? The metaphysical answer to either question depends on how you want to define the terms; since we are concerned with

*American Psychological Association. *Publication Manual of the American Psychological Association* (2nd ed.). Washington: Author, 1974.

†Schindler, G. E. Why engineers and scientists write as they do—Twelve characteristics of their prose. *IEEE Transactions on Engineering Writing and Speech*, 1967, *EWS-10*, 27–32.

‡Decker, B. Words about words, I. Pessimistic. *The Journal of Creative Behavior*, 1967, *1*, 34. Published by the Creative Education Foundation, Buffalo, New York. Reprinted by permission.

a practical answer, we can at least say that unreported research might as well not have been done. The ultimate goal of research is not doing experiments but building a scientific body of knowledge. If other scientists do not know about your experiments, your results cannot be used as building blocks. The experimental report is the way to make your results public so that science can benefit from your research.

Since your experimental report is the product of your research, you should try to make it a high-quality product. While an elegantly written experimental report cannot save a bad piece of research, a poorly written report can effectively destroy a good piece of research. I know researchers who, based on informal discussions of their research, seem to do well-thought-out experiments on important problems, but their ability to communicate on paper is so poor that their work is unknown. Much good research is probably lost this way.

Even instructors in writing courses have a difficult time teaching people how to write orderly thoughts, so the goal of this chapter is much more limited. I will describe the parts of a research report and give you some suggestions for determining whether what you write is readable.

Experimental reports should convey information efficiently. With this guideline in mind, the American Psychological Association has compiled a set of rules for writing an experimental report: the *Publication Manual of the American Psychological Association*.[1] A well-thumbed copy of this publication should sit on every experimental psychologist's desk. Even if you are writing an experimental report as a class project, you should follow the general guidelines in the *Publication Manual*. While we obviously cannot discuss all of the topics covered in the 136 pages of the manual, I will try to mention the most important rules and point out where new investigators often make mistakes.

PARTS OF A REPORT

All experimental reports should contain certain standard sections in proper order. Otherwise we would have to be like the old minister who said of his sermons: "First I tell 'em what I'm gonna tell 'em, then I tell 'em, then I tell 'em what I told 'em." Experimental reports all follow a standard pattern, so we do not need to use much space "telling 'em what we're gonna tell 'em." Not only does the standardized structure improve writing efficiency, but the consistent organization also allows the reader interested in only one section, such as the method or results, to quickly find that information. Here are the parts of a report in order.

Title

During the first two months after publication, about half of the research reports in major psychology journals are likely to be read by fewer than 200 psychologists.[2] The people who do read a report have probably selected it based on the title, since most psychologists regularly scan the title pages of several journals looking for current research that might interest them. Most of the key words used in a literature search (Chapter 3) are also chosen from the title. Thus, in some respects, the title is the most important part of your report; if your title conveys little information or the wrong information, you may lose most readers even before they know what you did.

The two most helpful suggestions for creating a title are contradictory: (1) Put in as much information as possible. (2) Make it as short as possible. Most titles should mention the major independent variables of interest and the dependent variable. You should also identify the general area of research if it is not obvious from the variables. The *Publication Manual* says that titles should be no longer than 12 to 15 words. Most titles should be considerably shorter than this.*

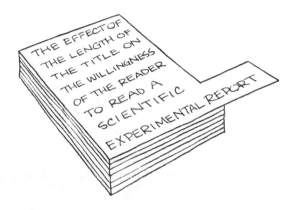

One way to create a title is to start with a long version and then eliminate words until you are absolutely unwilling to shorten it any further. As an example, suppose we needed a title for the print-size experiment we discussed earlier. As a first step we might start with this: *An experiment examining the effect of the size of print on the time to read a standard paragraph for children of various ages.* Now let's shorten it. We can immediately eliminate "An experiment examining the effect of . . . ," since these words give the reader no new information. We can also eliminate most of the prepositions (of, on, to, for) by rearranging the words. In this case, it is also more efficient to identify the specific levels of the independent variable (8- and 12-year-olds) than to use a general descriptor (children of various ages). After a little work, the title might read: *Print size and reading speed of 8- and 12-year-olds.* This title contains most of the original information but is certainly much shorter.

---

*Although I have no evidence to back it up, it seems to me that, in general, the better known the article, the shorter the title. Perhaps this effect is due to the memory span of the reader, or maybe good writers work at creating short titles. Perhaps I should have called this book *Book.*

Authors and Institution

After the title, list the author or authors, followed by the institution where the research was done. When there are multiple authors, list only those who have made substantial scientific contributions to the study. People who have simply helped collect or analyze some of the data should be acknowledged in a footnote rather than listed as an author. Generally the person who took primary responsibility for the research will also write the research report and should be listed as the first author. When several authors have made equal contributions, the order is sometimes determined by tossing a coin. When several reports are produced by the same team of investigators, first authorships are often passed around.

Abstract

The abstract is the second most important part of the report. Once an investigator chooses your paper because the title is of interest, he or she will next read the abstract, either in the journal or in *Psychological Abstracts*. Like a door-to-door salesperson, the title may get your foot in the door, but the abstract can get you an invitation into the house.

The abstract should be a condensed version of the complete report. Most investigators wait to write the abstract until the rest of the paper is finished, although it appears immediately after the title in the final report. In 100 to 175 words, you should introduce the problem, name the variables, briefly present the method, mention the important results, and discuss the implications of the results. As you can see, you must cover a lot of information in only a few words. Again, you may find it useful to write a long first draft of the abstract and then start eliminating unnecessary information and parts of speech. If the abstract is still too long after this first editing, you will have to make some choices about the relative importance of the remaining information, eliminating the least important material until your abstract meets the length requirements.

Some investigators treat titles and abstracts as afterthoughts. They dash them off after having taken great pains with the body of the paper. In this discussion, I have tried to convince you that the title and abstract are the two most important parts of your experimental report. Give them your best effort.

Introduction

The introduction is used to describe the current state of the body of knowledge. Since it is always the first section of the body of the report, you don't need a heading. You should assume that the reader has some familiarity with your area of research, so you only need to mention the few experiments most relevant to the one you have done.* Describe these key experiments in only enough detail to set the stage for your experiment. A good introduction is a mini-literature review that leaves your readers with the feeling that they know what experiment should be done next—the one you did.

After reviewing the supporting literature, you should state the purpose or object of your experiment. This statement should specify the relationship between the independent and dependent variables that you investigated. For example: "The purpose of this experiment was to de-

---

* A note about how to cite experiments: For one author, just give the author's name and the date of the article: "Jones (1967) found . . ." or "It was found (Jones, 1967). . . ." For two authors, use both last names: "Jones and Smith (1971) found . . . ," or "It was found (Jones & Smith, 1971) that . . . ." For more than two authors, use all of the names the first time you cite the research and the first author's name followed by "et al." thereafter: "Johnson et al. (1972) also found . . . ."

termine if print size would have the same effect on reading speed for 8-year-olds as for 12-year-olds." If you can predict the outcome of the experiment from the literature review or from a theoretical argument, do so here. You must explain the logic behind your prediction, however, since the purpose of predicting an outcome is to make the results easier to interpret later in the report. If your prediction is an unsupportable hunch, don't waste the reader's time.

Method

At this point, your readers should know why you did what you did. Now you must tell them what you did. The method section should contain enough detail so that the reader could replicate your experiment. However, you must use your judgment about which details are relevant to the experimental outcome. For example, in the print-size experiment, you would not need to specify the exact dimensions of the room in which the paragraphs were read, although you would certainly specify the dimensions of the paper each paragraph was typed on. Since it is impossible to mention each circumstance from the infinite set of circumstances, you should limit yourself to those that could logically have been expected to influence the results.

The method section is usually divided into several subsections. A typical report has three subsections, although you may wish to use additional subsections if your experiment calls for more.

Subjects. The subjects* subsection should specify who the subjects were: Were they students, pilots, children? What sex were they? How many subjects did you use, and how did you select them? (Were they volunteers? Were they satisfying a class requirement? Were they paid?) If you eliminated the data for any subjects (see Chapter 5), you should indicate the basis for this decision. For animal subjects, be sure to report their genus and species along with their age and sex.

Apparatus. The apparatus section should describe the equipment or materials you used in your experiment. If you used a standard psychological apparatus, you need only give the general name, the manufacturer, and the model number ("A Scientific Prototype two-channel tachistoscope, Model 800-F, was used ..."). Describe any custom-built apparatus in enough detail so that the reader could construct a similar apparatus ("The slides were back-projected on a Plexiglas panel 15 cm high and 20 cm wide, mounted vertically 30 cm from the

---

* When reading experimental reports published prior to 1974, you will see the word *subject* abbreviated as *S* and *experimenter* as *E*. These abbreviations are no longer acceptable. In fact, you should try to use a more descriptive word than *subjects* if possible, such as "students," "children," or "rats."

subject.")* Be sure to make a note of all the measurements at the time you do the experiment. Reconstructing these details after the experiment is often difficult and sometimes impossible.

Procedure.   The procedure section should specify exactly what happened to each subject during the experiment. You can paraphrase instructions to the subject to save space unless the type of instructions was an independent variable. Explain the experimental design along with any randomization and counterbalancing procedures.

Results

You should report the results of most experiments using one or more descriptive statistics. Provide raw data only when illustrating a general finding or when showing the results of baseline experiments. Whenever you report a measure of central tendency, such as the mean, you should usually include a measure of dispersion as well, such as the standard deviation. If you mention only a few measures, you can include them in the text: "The response times for the 1-, 2-, and 4-sec foreperiods were 350, 362, and 391 msec, respectively." However, use a table or figure when you must report many measures.

Investigators typically use tables to show the results of main effects and when exact values of the dependent variable are necessary. You should type tables on separate pages from the text, with the instruction "Insert Table 1 about here" typed in the text to indicate the approximate location for the table. The short sample report in Appendix B shows how a table should generally be organized. For specific problems, you will have to refer to the *Publication Manual*.

Use figures sparingly, for they are even more costly to draw and print than are tables.† As we saw in Chapter 9, however, figures are a great way to show interactions and to illustrate trends in the data. Here are some general rules to follow in drawing figures:

1. Label the abscissa and ordinate, and specify the units of measurement.‡
2. Draw the ordinate about two-thirds as long as the abscissa.
3. Make 0 the smallest mark on the ordinate. If you must break the ordinate to save space (for example, if you have no response times between 0 and .3 second), indicate the break by a double slashed line at that point.
4. Use point and line codes (as in Figure 9-8) to indicate those independent variables not listed on the abscissa. Make these codes consistent

---

* Report all measurements in metric units. If the object was manufactured in nonmetric units, report them as such but insert the metric equivalents in parentheses ("The panel was 3 ft (.91 m) in width.").

† A figure is any visual representation of data that cannot be set in standard type. Graphs are the most common figures in experimental reports.

‡ New investigators commonly forget this step. To avoid this error, set a rule for yourself that you will never put in a data point until you have labeled the axes.

throughout the report. Do not rely on different colors to make your distinctions. Colors should be used only in coloring books!

5. Draw your figures on pages separate from the text, and indicate the location of figures by putting "Insert Figure 1 about here" in the text.

These rules are designed to help you make your results clear and to minimize the possibility of distortion. You may find, however, that you will need to bend them occasionally to keep from distorting your data.

The results of inferential statistical tests are reported in a standard way. For example, if the result of a t test* done on two groups of ten subjects was 4.7, which you found to be significant at the .01 level, you would report it as follows: "The difference between groups was found to be significant, $\underline{t}$ (18) = 4.7, $\underline{p}$ < .01."† Report other tests in the same way, first stating the symbol for the test statistic (underlined if not a Greek letter), followed by the degrees of freedom in parentheses, an equals sign, the result of the test calculation, a comma, a lowercase $\underline{p}$ underlined for italic, a < sign (or, for nonsignificant results, a > sign), and finally the testing level. When the results of a statistical test are very complex, you may want to put them in a table.

No interpretation of the results, other than information needed for clarification, should be done in the results section. Some investigators, however, prefer to combine the results and discussion sections under one heading, which is legitimate when it allows you to present the information more clearly or more efficiently.

Discussion

In your introduction you described what the body of knowledge consisted of and where it needed to be expanded. Your results section then provided a new building block.‡ You now have to describe how the new block fits the structure and how the new structure differs from the old. Thus, the discussion section is the place where you update the body of knowledge with your results.

This section is also the place to qualify your results, if necessary, and to speculate on the reasons for unpredicted findings (as long as you keep your speculations short and identify them as such). However, you should not waste the reader's time explaining effects that were not statistically significant. Only in rare cases should negative results be interpreted as due to anything other than chance.

---

*A t test is an inferential test that indicates whether the means of two samples are significantly different from each other. The result of a t test is a number. By comparing this number with other numbers listed in a table, you can determine if the means are statistically different at a particular probability level (for example, a probability level of .01, p < .01).

† The number in parentheses is the degrees of freedom for the t test. Most statistical tests have a degrees-of-freedom term, either a single number or two numbers. You will find out how to determine this number when you learn those tests.

‡ Or, in some cases, your experiment may have blasted away part of the existing structure.

Particularly if you are doing applied work, you should use the discussion section to point out the practical value of your results—how and where they can be used and how they might change current applied procedures.

Finally, you can use the discussion section to make suggestions about the direction of future research. Now that you have discussed the new state of the body of knowledge, you may be able to suggest where new expansion should take place.

References

Your reference section should list only those references cited in the report and should be ordered alphabetically by the first author's name. The references listed at the end of each chapter in this book and in the sample report (Appendix B) follow the proper style and should provide you with many useful examples. For unusual references, refer to the *Publication Manual*.

WRITING STYLE

Experimental reports are not intended to be literary masterpieces or entertaining monologues. Thus, your general writing style should not get in the way of smoothly flowing thoughts, nor should it bring more attention to you than to your research. In order to meet these requirements, scientific writing has evolved a standard style.

Traditionally, scientific writers have used third-person passive voice rather than first-person active. Instead of writing "I did this experiment in order to . . .," the investigator would write "This experiment was done in order to . . . ." While this style did keep the report from reading like a letter home, it also forced out much of its life. The prose became dull and monotonous and caused the reader more pain than pleasure. Today it is considered proper to use the pronoun "I" to a limited extent: for example, "I thought that . . ." rather than "It was thought that . . . ." You should, however, avoid excessive use of "I" to keep from drawing the reader's attention to you rather than to the research. You should also try to use an active verb form rather than a passive form, especially when there are no pronoun problems—for example, "A previous report described a new method" rather than "In a previous report, a new method was described."* Again the general rule is to use words that make the writing come alive without interrupting the smooth flow of thoughts.

The context of a sentence will usually tell you which verb tense to use. Most sentences in the introduction and method sections refer to past actions ("Boles (1972) reported . . ." and "The subjects recalled the words . . ."). On the other hand, results "are" and theory "is" even after the experiment is completed. That is, the body of knowledge exists in the present and so should be discussed using present-tense verbs ("These data support an interference theory of forgetting.").

Finally, scientific writing should be concise. The limited resources of time and space simply do not allow us the luxury of excess verbiage. For instance, the style I have used in this book would not be appropriate for scientific writing.† I have purposely used more words than necessary because I have tried to do more than transfer information; I have tried to convince, cajole, and convert you as well as communicate with you. In scientific writing, you should assume that the reader has already been convinced, cajoled, and converted; your only job then is to communicate.

The most common problem new investigators have with report writing is laziness. The investigator is not really lazy, of course, since lazy people do not do experiments, but his or her writing style may be lazy. In writing a report, the most important end of your pencil is the one without the point. It is an extremely rare person who can sit down at a typewriter and write a good, concise report the first time through. Most good scientific writers have to try a number of alternative words and sentence structures before deciding on the best one. Every word must say precisely what you want it to say, and every sentence should flow smoothly into the next. Writing this way is hard work!

When writing a report, most investigators first produce a draft of the best version they are capable of. Getting the report to this point may take two or three drafts, since it is often easier to rewrite whole sections than to make corrections on top of corrections. Once you come up with a final draft you are satisfied with, you should give it to several people to read. At least one of these people should be unfamiliar with your experiment since you are probably so familiar with your own research that you cannot judge how well the report describes it. Since you already

---

*Some writers may object to this form on the grounds that a report cannot describe—an author describes. I suppose writing is largely a matter of personal preference. In this case, I prefer to trade a little accuracy for a lot livelier style.

†If I had written the book in scientific style, you would have been bored, I would have been bored, and the publisher would have been bored. My mother would have bought the only copy; she loves me even when I'm boring.

know what happened, your mind conveniently fills in all the gaps you leave in the report. An uninformed reader can be a good gap detector.*

AN ENEMY MAKES THE BEST CRITIC.

It is also helpful to give the report to a reader who is familiar with what you did so that he or she can tell you whether you did what you said you did. This person can serve as your error detector. Finally, you should have a reader who is familiar with scientific writing style and is a good writer. This reader can tell you how you might improve the way you say what you did.

After getting comments from these readers, you are ready to write a final version of the report. This copy should be neatly typed and proof-read before you submit it.

Some of you may find that if you follow the procedure I have been describing, your reports will be more readable; others may find that another procedure works best. Writing is an art; what works for one writer may not work for another. However, the major point we have been discussing is valid for any procedure: the report is the final product of your research and deserves at least the same effort you give to all of the other aspects of your research.

SUMMARY

Since research is worthless unless other scientists know about it, experimenters must make their results known by writing a high-quality experimental report. This report should follow the guidelines recommended by the American Psychological Association in their *Publication Manual*. A report has standardized sections. Since many readers will

---

*On the death of one of his scientific colleagues, one of my friends remarked to me: "I'm really going to miss him. He was one of my best enemies. Now I don't know who I'll send my reports to." It is often best to have someone read your report who will go ahead and be critical without fearing that he or she will break up a social relationship. Friends are often too nice to be good critics.

decide whether to read a report on the basis of its *title,* it should be short but convey enough information to help the reader make this decision. The *authors* and the *institution* where the research was done should follow the title. The *abstract,* a short (100 to 175 words) version of the complete report, follows.

In the body of the report, the *introduction* should review enough literature to give the reader an idea of the current state of the body of knowledge and should state the purpose of the experiment. The *method* section provides the reader with the information necessary to replicate the experiment. It is typically divided into three subsections: *subjects,* which describes the type and number of subjects and how they were recruited; *apparatus,* which gives others the information necessary to order or build the equipment and materials similar to those used; and *procedure,* which should give a detailed account of what happened to each subject. The *results* section summarizes the findings of the experiment using descriptive and inferential statistics along with tables and figures. The report writer then relates results back to the body of knowledge in the *discussion* section. The report concludes with an alphabetical list of the *references* cited in the paper.

In order to convey information as efficiently as possible while keeping the general writing style lively, it is no longer necessary to write experimental reports exclusively in third-person passive voice. Active verbs are now considered preferable, and occasional use of first person is acceptable. The introduction and method sections are typically written in past tense, while present tense is appropriate for the results and discussion sections. Since the report should be as concise as possible, you should avoid lazy writing and use the comments of other readers to make the report a high-quality product.

REFERENCES

1. American Psychological Association. *Publication manual of the American Psychological Association* (2nd ed.). Washington, D. C.: Author, 1974.
2. Garvey, W. D., & Griffith, B. C. Scientific communication: Its role in the conduct of research and creation of knowledge. *American Psychologist,* 1971, *26,* 349–362.

How to Use Theory

11

Einstein told me how, since his boyhood, he thought about the man running after the light ray and the man closed in a falling elevator. The picture of the man running after the light ray led to special relativity theory. The picture of the man in a falling elevator led to general relativity theory.[*]

Holmes—"I have no data yet. It is a capital mistake to theorize before one has data. Insensibly one begins to twist facts to suit theories, instead of theories to suit facts."[†]

As disappointing as it may sound after having just read most of a book telling you how to do experiments, doing experiments is only part of doing science. Throughout the book we have been referring to experiments as building blocks used for constructing a scientific body of knowledge. Just as a randomly arranged pile of blocks is not a building, so a randomly arranged collection of experiments is not a science. In either case, we need a blueprint as well. In science, a blueprint is called a *theory.*

In fact, one of the reasons experimental psychology is more fun than some of the other sciences is that experimental psychologists can be architects as well as builders. Other sciences have imposed a division of labor. For instance, most physicists are either theoretical physicists or experimental physicists, but not both. Experimental psychologists have traditionally done both jobs.

TYPES OF THEORIES

Definitions of theory tend to be so general that they are not very instructive. However, if forced to define *theory,* I would say that a theory is a partially verified statement of a scientific relationship that cannot be

[*] Infeld, L. *Albert Einstein.* New York: Charles Scribners, 1950. p. 48.
[†] Doyle, Arthur Conan, "A Scandal in Bohemia."

EXPERIMENTAL PSYCHOLOGISTS DO TWO JOBS.

directly observed. The qualification that a relationship not be observable stems from the fact that theoretical relationships are often between general categories of circumstances or behaviors rather than specific instances. For example, the theoretical statement that viewing violence causes aggression is different from an experimental demonstration that children seeing a war movie choose to play with guns. Other theoretical statements may not be observable because they concern internal processes, such as the theory that some people remember words by forming mental pictures. In some cases the state of technology will not allow the theory to be verified by observation—for example, the theory that learning specific tasks causes predictable structural changes in RNA.

Theories can take many forms. In this chapter we will discuss three types of theories* and illustrate them using the question "Does violence on TV cause aggression?"

Descriptive Theories

A *descriptive theory* simply attaches names to events without necessarily explaining why or how the events have occurred. For example, Freud, as part of psychoanalytic theory, said that repression occurs when we unconsciously refuse to admit painful or disagreeable ideas to conscious thought. While such a theory may help clinicians in their work, the mere naming does little to explain the conditions under which repression occurs or how we might examine it experimentally. In a similar way, psychologists interested in motivation were enraptured with naming instincts for many years. At first the concept of an instinct seemed to be quite useful, since it appeared that most animal behaviors could be classified as reflecting certain instincts (such as the feeding instinct or the mating instinct). However, eventually psychologists began to ac-

---

*The three types of theories discussed here are similar to those mentioned by Arnoult in his book *Scientific Method in Psychology,* although some of the names have been changed.[1]

cumulate as many names for instincts as there were observable behaviors (such as the "running into a hole when attacked from the front" instinct), and the concept lost its usefulness.

Descriptive theories can be useful, however, if the names are attached to operationally definable classes of events rather than to individually observable events. For example, we might state that observing violence causes aggressive behavior. If we could operationally define *violence* and *aggressive behavior* as general classes of events, we might have a useful descriptive theory. However, even this kind of descriptive theory is of limited value because it does not explain how the relationship works.

A DESCRIPTIVE THEORY

Analogical Theories

Analogical theories explain how relationships work by drawing an analogy between a psychological relationship and a physical model so that the physical analog becomes a psychological model of behavior. For example, many of the theories that attempt to explain how humans process information use the computer as a physical analog. Of course, nobody believes that the brain works exactly like a computer, but there are enough similarities that computer modeling has provided some very useful analogical theories.

As an example of an analogical theory, let's take the physical properties of inertia as an analog for the relationship between violence and aggression. As you may know, a physical object has inertia in proportion to its speed and weight; the faster it is traveling and the heavier it is, the more inertia it has. This inertia can be overcome by friction. Thus, an analogical theory relating violence and aggression might be stated this way: "The amount of aggression expressed by an observer is like the force exerted by a moving object, where the degree of violence observed is analogous to the weight of the object and the time of observing is analogous to the speed of the object. After exposure to violence, the aggressive tendencies will decrease in the same way that friction overcomes inertia."

This analogical theory is more useful than the descriptive theory proposed in the previous section because it explains some of the complexities of the relationship. We should also be able to test the theory based on our knowledge of how the physical model works. For example, we know that the longer a force is exerted on a physical object, the faster its speed and the greater its inertia. Thus, a longer time is needed for friction to overcome the inertia. By analogy, the longer a person observes violence, the longer it would take the aggressive tendencies to disappear.

AN ANALOGICAL THEORY

Because of its explanatory power, an analogical theory is certainly more useful than a descriptive theory. However, analogical theories are also doomed to failure in the end, for at some point the properties of the physical analog will no longer correspond to the properties of the human. For this reason, you can best use analogical theories as first approximations that help you identify the major variables and outline in a general way how the variables affect one another. However, you will find that analogical theories are seldom powerful enough to help you specify the exact mathematical relationships among the variables.

Quantitative Theories

Quantitative theories do attempt to state relationships in mathematical terms. They specify not only the direction of relationships among categories of variables but also how these categories are quantitatively related. Few psychological theories have reached this level of sophistication. Only a few subareas in learning, memory, and information processing have attempted to use quantitative theories.

Quantitative theories have been limited in psychology because psychologists have more difficulty with variability than do physical scientists. For example, in physics the theory of gravity is a quantitative theory expressed in precise mathematical terms. Since gravity affects all physical objects in the same way, a physicist can assume that any variability in experimental results is simply a measurement error. In psychology, however, we cannot predict how all subjects will behave based on one subject's behavior, nor can we predict how the same subject will behave at any given time. Consequently, our quantitative theories must be able to accommodate variability. The best we can do is to predict how probable it is that a behavior will occur,* so we must express mathematical relationships in probabilistic terms (for example, the probability that a subject will learn this list of words in five trials is .8).

Psychologists also face the problem of deciding what scale to use in measuring behaviors. In the physical sciences, the units for measuring speed or mass are not controversial. In psychology, however, we have to find scales by which we can measure such concepts as violence or aggression. For example, consider the following quantitative theory: humans express a level of aggressiveness in direct proportion to the average level of violence they have observed. Since our proposed theory attempts to establish a mathematical relationship between the scales of violence and aggression, we must first determine how to measure them. As you can see, establishing scales for such concepts is no easy task.

A QUANTITATIVE THEORY

As a result of these problems, most theories in psychology are still descriptive or analogical. However, as psychology becomes more sophisticated and we learn to handle the difficulties caused by variability and scaling, more psychological theories will become quantitative.

---

* In some areas, physical scientists must now deal with similar problems. The structure of atoms, for example, is now expressed probabilistically.

PROPERTIES OF A GOOD THEORY

How do you know a good theory when you see one? In the last section I implied that quantitative theories were better than analogical theories, which in turn were better than descriptive theories. Why is this true?

First, a theory must be able to *account for most of the data* already collected. There is no use proposing a theory if the data do not support it. (You can see why a thorough literature search is so important; it will allow you to eliminate some of the competing theories prior to collecting any data.) One or two items of disconfirming evidence, however, will usually not destroy a theory unless there is an alternative theory that can account for all of the evidence. We will discuss how experimental results affect theory later in the chapter.

A theory must also be *testable*. If a theory is so universal that it can account for any experimental result, then it is impossible to prove it or disprove it. For example, Freud's theory of repression is virtually untestable as it is usually stated. How could you disprove repression experimentally? Perhaps you could provide subjects with an experience they would rather forget. For instance, you might tempt subjects to cheat and then confront those who succumbed with their dreadful deed.* Sometime later you might have a close friend of each subject ask whether he or she had ever cheated. If no subjects report having cheated, you have support for the theory, since it shows that all of the subjects repressed the incident. However, if all subjects report having cheated, this result doesn't eliminate the theory, since the theory never claimed that all people repress a particular event, only that some people sometimes repress some events. Thus, your experiment would do little to dislodge the theory. A theory that is so general that no test can be proposed to discredit it is a worthless theory from a scientific point of view.

While a theory should not be so general that it can account for any behavior, it should also *not be too restrictive*. That is, the fewer directly observable events the theory can account for, the less valuable it is. In the most extreme case, a theory would simply restate the relationship between observable events.† For example, the statement that "8-year-old children hit a punching bag more after watching a televised 'Roadrunner' cartoon" is less useful than the statement that "Watching violence on TV causes aggression in children." Even more useful is the statement that "observing violence causes people to be more aggressive." The more general our statements, the more valuable they are because they account for a larger set of observable events.

Finally, a good theory will *predict* the outcome of future experiments. Even descriptive theories specify the relationship between categories of events. Thus, the relationships between directly observable events that are members of these categories are predictable from the

---

* Let's ignore for the moment whether this experiment would be considered ethical.
† Actually such a statement would not fit our definition of a theory, but some investigators would call it a theory.

theory. Analogical and quantitative theories also allow you to predict the relationships between events and these predictions are even more precise.

A GOOD THEORY ALLOWS YOU TO PREDICT...

WHAT IS A THEORY GOOD FOR?

Why does science need theories? What are they good for? B. F. Skinner has a concise answer to this question; he says they are good for nothing.[2] Skinner maintains that theories do more harm than good, for three major reasons.

First, he states that our job as psychologists is to account for observable events and that since theories are more abstract than the observable events, they really do not help us to account for them. Second, since theories seem to explain events that we haven't observed as well as those we have observed, they can lull us into believing that our research is complete when we have much left to do. We are tempted to use theories to fill in the holes in our research without really knowing whether the answers the theories give us are true. Finally, Skinner points out that when we let a theory guide our research and then this theory is overthrown, we lose much of the research generated by the theory. He argues that good research is good research independent of any theory.

Skinner's position has some merit (we will return to some of his points at the end of the chapter), but most psychologists disagree with him and feel that theories are vital to research. What do they think theories are good for?

We have already discussed one of the major purposes of theory: it helps to *organize the data*. Studying data isolated from theory is about as interesting as reading the closing quotations from the New York Stock Exchange if you don't own any shares. By categorizing directly observable events and saying how the categories are related, a theory provides a meaningful way to organize our knowledge.

By organizing data, a theory also suggests *possible directions for future research*. If you randomly arranged half of the raw materials needed to build a house in front of you and someone asked you "What do you need next?" you would probably have a tough time answering the question. But if you could take a blueprint and construct as much of the house as possible, you would have a way of determining what materials were missing. A theory provides a similar function for science. Even if the theory is somewhat vague, or if there are several competing theories, it can provide enough organization to indicate which variables we should investigate and which relationships we should look for.

Theory can also be valuable for *providing answers to applied problems*. For example, suppose you work for a TV network, and somebody has proposed a new children's show. You want to know whether this show will make the children watching it more aggressive and, if so, how much more aggressive. You could take 100 children, expose them to a pilot show, and somehow measure their aggressiveness, but this procedure would be expensive and time-consuming. Further, you would have to repeat the experiment every time another new show was proposed. However, if we had a theory specifying which dimensions make a TV show violent and predicting how these dimensions affect children's aggressiveness, we could use the theory in place of direct observation, or at least we could use the theory to reduce the amount of data we would need to collect. The theory might tell us which dimensions need to be experimentally investigated.

Thus, theory can reduce the number of experiments we need to do in applied research. And in many cases a theory will give a close enough approximation to an experimental result that the theoretical prediction can be used in place of it.

TESTING THEORIES

We discussed earlier that good theories must be testable, but how do we go about testing them? Obviously we must do experiments, and somehow the results of these experiments must tell us something about whether the theory is true.

In deciding whether a theory is true, we must make an inference. If the evidence leading to a conclusion allows us to infer that one and only one conclusion could be true, then we call our inference *deductive*. For example: if all mammals are animals and a horse is a mammal, then a horse is an animal. There is no uncertainty about the outcome of this deductive inference or any deductive inference.

We must make *inductive* inferences in the face of uncertainty, however. We make an inductive inference when the evidence supports a particular conclusion only probabilistically. For example: if most men have deep voices and Pat has a deep voice, then Pat is *probably* a man. We can state that the outcome is true only in probabilistic terms.

We must distinguish between deductive and inductive inferences in order to see how experimental results affect theories. Suppose we wanted to test the analogical theory mentioned earlier, that observing violence affects a person's aggressiveness the way inertia affects a physical object. The first step would be to determine (or to deduce, since, as we will see, this is a deductive inference) some consequences of this theory. Consequence A might be that subjects observing very violent situations become very aggressive. Consequence B might be that subjects exposed to violent situations for long periods of time are more aggressive than those exposed for only a short time. Consequence C might be that subjects exposed to violence for longer periods of time are aggressive for a longer time after exposure.

Since each of these consequences can be directly observed, we can test them by doing experiments. Suppose we do three appropriate experiments to test these consequences and find that Consequences A and B are true and C is false. What can we conclude about the theory?

Figure 11-1 illustrates the steps we have taken. From the theory at the top, we inferred three directly observable consequences. This inference was deductive: if the theory is true, then the consequences must be true. Then we did an experiment to test each consequence and found two of them to be true and the third to be false. Now we must make another inference as to the truth of the theory.

The two true consequences obviously support the theory, but they do so in an inductive way; that is, they increase our confidence in the theory, but they do not eliminate the possibility that the theory is false. The more consequences of the theory we find to be true, the more probable it is that the theory is indeed true. However, using this process of inference, we can never be absolutely sure about the truth of a theory. You can see why I cringe when an investigator claims "My experiment *proves* that the theory is true." The inferential process simply does not allow such a statement to be made. A positive result can never prove a theory true. The investigator would have a stronger claim (although

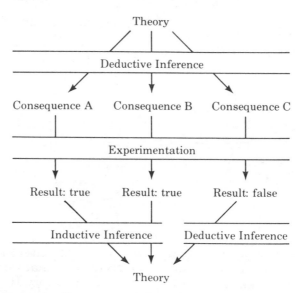

Figure 11–1.   An illustration of the deductive and inductive links relating experimentation to theory.

still not quite accurate) if he said that a negative result proved the theory to be false. Why is this?

The basic rules of logic say that a theory can be disproven if a consequence is false. Because a consequence is deductively inferred from a theory, we know that if the theory is true, the consequence must be true. Thus, if we do an experiment showing that the consequence is false, we can deductively infer that the theory must also be false. From a logical point of view, then, we can disprove a theory. However, we have forgotten one of the things we learned in Chapter 9. When a test statistic exceeds a critical value that is determined by the level of significance, we infer that the chances the samples came from the same population are small. Thus, a significant result tells us that the data samples probably came from different populations. Yet experimentally demonstrating that a consequence is false usually involves showing conditions to be equivalent rather than different, and, since we do not have statistical tests that will do this, we have to be very careful in concluding that the consequence is false.

To use an example, Consequence C of the inertia theory is that the longer a subject is exposed to violence, the longer the aggression will last. To test this consequence, suppose we do an experiment in which we expose one group of subjects to 1 hour of violent TV, another group to 2 hours, and a third to 4 hours. We then measure how long each group's aggressiveness lasts and find that there are no significant differences among the groups. Can we therefore declare the theory to be false? Not with absolute certainty, because the statistical test we used gave us only the probability that the differences we found could have been due to chance. The test cannot tell us how likely it is that the groups are equivalent.

Even if we could have shown the consequence to be false by testing in the proper direction (that is, by determining that the consequence is false because an effect is significant), we could still be in error. If we tested at the .05 level, for example, we could expect to be wrong 1 time in 20. So even in this case the strong deductive links that could allow us to disprove a theory are weakened by the inductive inference we make when interpreting the experimental results.*

It is not necessary for you to analyze the logical basis for every experiment you do. However, it is important for you to understand in a general way how experimentation interacts with theory. Hopefully this discussion will help you appreciate why it is necessary to do many experiments in order to gain confidence in or lose confidence in (not prove or disprove) any theory.

DOES THEORY ALWAYS PRECEDE DATA?

In our somewhat idealized discussion of the relationship between theories and experiments, we have been pretending that we first propose a theory and then do experiments to evaluate the theory. However, many investigators prefer to model themselves after Sherlock Holmes: only after collecting all possible clues (data) will they nail the culprit (theory). They feel that proposing a theory before collecting data is like deciding on the villain and then looking for clues related only to that person's guilt; both procedures are biased. We have already learned Skinner's opinion on this matter. Perhaps he stated it best when he wrote "There are doubtless many men whose curiosity about nature is less than their curiosity about the accuracy of their guesses. . . ."[4]

Many investigators believe that research should be done because a problem exists. They collect data and then propose a theory to account for the data and solve the problem. There is certainly some merit in this position, because research motivated by theory as opposed to research motivated by a problem has some notable drawbacks. Perhaps the most serious drawback is that investigators often propose theories for easily solvable problems rather than for important problems. Since no science has the resources to investigate all problems, we must choose, and we obviously should choose important problems to work on. If, because of theories, we choose to investigate easy but rather unimportant problems instead of more difficult but important problems, we may be misusing our resources.† In order to counteract this problem, I have threatened at times to teach a course entitled *Psych 371—Things Psychology Knows Nothing About.* The purpose of this course would be to find important

---

*For a more detailed discussion of these issues, see Chapters 12–14 of McGuigan's *Experimental Psychology, A Methodological Approach.*[3]

† Kuhn in his book *The Structure of Scientific Revolutions*[5] argues, in fact, that once the scientific community has accepted a paradigm (a set of assumptions or a widely accepted model), scientists then work only on problems that can be assumed to have solutions within that paradigm. "To a great extent these are the only problems that the community will admit as scientific . . . . A paradigm can, for that matter, even insulate the community from those socially important problems that are not reducible to the puzzle form, because they cannot be stated in terms of the conceptual and instrumental tools the paradigm supplies."

areas of human behavior that nobody is currently investigating and to propose how one might begin research in these areas.

A rational position probably lies somewhere between the theory-driven position and the problem-driven position. We should certainly be concerned with choosing important problems to work on, but we should not turn our backs on theories as excellent vehicles for organizing and directing research on these problems.

SUMMARY

As scientists, psychologists not only do experiments but also use theories to build a scientific body of knowledge. A *theory,* which is defined as a partially verified statement of a scientific relationship that cannot be directly observed, can be of three types. A *descriptive theory* attaches names to events and is most useful when the names are attached to operationally definable classes of events. *Analogical theories* explain how relationships work by drawing an analogy between the psychological relationship and a physical model. *Quantitative theories* specify relationships in mathematical terms. Psychology has very few quantitative theories, since we are still learning how to account for variability and how to develop precise scales of measurement.

A good theory *accounts for most of the data,* is *testable,* is *not too restrictive,* and is able to *predict* the outcome of future experiments. Skinner feels that theories are useless because they do not help account for observable events, they lull us into believing unfinished research is complete, and they lead to research that becomes useless when the theory is overthrown. Most investigators disagree, however. They believe that theories are useful because they *help to organize data, suggest possible directions for future research,* and *provide answers to applied problems.*

In testing theories, it is important to distinguish between *deductive inference,* in which the outcome is known with complete certainty, and *inductive inference,* in which the outcome is probabilistic. A theory leads deductively to certain consequences that can be experimentally tested. Those consequences found to be true increase our confidence in the theory through a process of inductive inference. The rules of logic say that a false consequence should cause us to deductively reject the theory, but since the inferential statistical tests we use are inductive, rejecting a theory is also an inductive process.

Although investigators usually propose a theory before collecting data, many investigators feel that we should first have a problem, then collect data, and finally construct a theory. They argue that this order of events leads to research that investigates important problems rather than research that investigates easy but unimportant problems.

REFERENCES

1. Arnoult, M. D. *Fundamentals of scientific method in psychology.* Dubuque, Iowa: William C. Brown, 1972.

2. Skinner, B. F. Are theories of learning necessary? *Psychological Review,* 1950, *57,* 193–216.
3. McGuigan, F. J. *Experimental psychology: A methodological approach* (2nd ed.). Englewood Cliffs, N. J.: Prentice-Hall, 1968.
4. Skinner, B. F. *The behavior of organisms.* New York: Appleton-Century-Crofts, 1938. P. 44.
5. Kuhn, T. S. *The structure of scientific revolutions* (2nd ed.). Chicago: University of Chicago Press, 1970.

Epilog

Congratulations on having wended your way through my thoughts on doing psychology experiments. I hope my words and pictures helped to hold your interest rather than obstruct your progress. There is a delicate balance between informality and precision, a balance that varies from one reader to another. Hopefully my prose was not too unbalanced for you.

Obviously this book has not instantly transformed you into a full-blown experimental psychologist, but I hope it has given you enough information so that you can attempt some simple experiments on your own. You will find that doing experiments is a lot more fun than reading about doing experiments. So now go have some fun!

How to Use Specialized Sources for a Literature Search

SCIENCE CITATION INDEX

To be thorough in your literature search, you can tree forward through the references as well as backward. For example, if you find a key article that is several years old and want to find more recent articles that have referenced that article, you can use the *Science Citation Index*. This journal is published quarterly and cumulated annually by the Institute for Scientific Information. Each year of the Index takes up a shelf in the library, since there are more than five million citations in this publication each year. It includes references from every article in over 2400 science journals. Since only about 100 of these journals are psychology journals, you will find about 95% of the information useless for your purposes.

After you get the hang of the abbreviation system, you will find the *Science Citation Index* fairly easy to use. Suppose that key article you found is five years old. You would first find the shelf that contains the *Citation Index* for the year following publication of the article and get the volume that lists the part of the alphabet containing your author's name. Look through the alphabetical listing of names until you find your author's name and initials. Notice that articles by several people with the same name may be listed under this heading.* Look for a listing of your key article. If it is not there, you can assume that nobody cited it during this year. If your article is listed, you will find a list of author's names and journals. These references are for articles that cited your key article. Write them down. Then repeat this process for each year up to the most recent, and you will have found every article that included the key article as a reference.

---

*For example, whenever I look up my listing, I can find out what my father, who is a physicist, has been doing. He is also D. W. Martin.

You can also recycle yourself by finding each article that cited the original article and then treeing backward using the references for each of these new articles. You may wish to take some of these newly acquired references, use them as key references, and go forward again. You can continue this process until you feel you have covered all of the important references.

HOW TO RECYCLE YOURSELF

AUTOMATED SEARCHES

If you have a grant that sponsors your research, or if you are independently wealthy, there are now some shortcuts to doing a literature search—*automated searches*. PASAR is an automatic-retrieval service provided by the American Psychological Association. All of the listings from *Psychological Abstracts* since 1967 have been put into a computer and indexed by author and subject descriptors. You can request a PASAR search by filling out a request form obtained from the American Psychological Association or found in *Psychological Abstracts* or the *American Psychologist*. You provide a narrative statement of your search topic, such as "the effects of foreperiod, stimulus intensity, or stimulus duration on reaction-time responses." You have to be a little careful how you phrase this statement. For example, if I had used "and" rather than "or" in the above statement, I would have meant that an experiment had to manipulate all of those variables to be selected. Fortunately, the service will usually contact you to make sure exactly what you want.

You must also list words or phrases that indicate the independent variables of prime importance. In the above example, I might put "foreperiod length, simple reaction time, choice reaction time, stimulus intensity, stimulus loudness, stimulus brightness, stimulus duration, stimulus length." This way I would be sure to get all of the research, even though it might be classified under many different descriptors. You will also provide a list of dependent-variable descriptors on the request form, such as "reaction time, latencies, response accuracy." After checking with you to be sure what you want to search, the people at PASAR will feed this information into their computer, which will then go through a search process similar to the one we described earlier. You will receive a copy and a carbon of each relevant listing from *Psychological Abstracts,* ordered alphabetically by author or chronologically by year, depending on what you request.

An automated search takes very little of your time, and it is fast. You get printed references and abstracts appropriate for filing with no mistakes; you get just what you asked for.

There are also several disadvantages of an automated search. You do get just what you asked for, but sometimes it's hard to know quite what to ask for. When you are doing the search by hand, you sometimes find out what you are searching for while you are searching. An automated search requires that you specify exactly what you are looking for prior to the search. A second disadvantage is that once you get the results of the automated search, you still have not completed the search process. You still have to sort the listings and examine the original articles. The final disadvantage is the worst: a search will cost you from $40 to $60 or more.*

While we are on the subject of money, here is a final word on how poor people like us can get free journal articles. When authors get articles published, they usually order 100 or so reprints of the article from the journal. As long as these reprints last, the author will send one to you if you ask nicely. The usual way is to send a postcard saying "I would very much appreciate receiving a reprint of your article entitled _____ that appeared in _____." Be sure to include your address. The author will send you a copy as a professional courtesy. Don't be embarrassed to send out these *reprint requests.* Many younger investigators who are trying to become familiar with research in a particular area but do not have the resources to buy their own journals send out reprint requests.

TECHNICAL REPORTS

Technical reports are often ignored as a source of psychological literature, but they can be helpful in certain areas of research. When the federal government supports research, particularly Defense Department research, the investigator is usually required to report it in the form of a technical report. This report is similar to a journal article but usually goes into more detail about the procedure and the apparatus, and sometimes it even lists the data. Technical reports are automatically distributed by the supporting governmental agency to other investigators who are doing similar research supported by that agency.

About one author in ten produces these technical reports, and only about one-third of these reports are later published in a journal.[1] Most libraries do not routinely order technical reports since they would

---

*Maybe I call this the worst disadvantage due to my Scots blood. Since I'm also half Irish, I usually go ahead and spend the money; I just get hostile afterward.

quickly fill up the shelves and are difficult for a library to organize and classify systematically. Investigators who are working on defense grants or contracts get a monthly publication listing abstracts of all technical reports. *Psychological Abstracts* also lists many of these reports. Unfortunately, technical reports are often difficult to obtain. To purchase them, you must send to the Defense Documentation Center in Alexandria, Virginia, and you must know the document number and the price of the report you want.

Recently a new publication of the American Psychological Association called *JSAS Catalog of Selected Documents in Psychology* has been formed to aid in the distribution of technical reports. This journal, which is put out by the Journal Supplement Abstract Service, lists manuscripts too lengthy for normal journal publication. The catalog lists each report in a form similar to that of *Psychological Abstracts* and indicates the price of the complete report. You can order any report listed directly from JSAS for this amount. Since authors must still submit the reports for review by a ten-member panel of editors, many technical reports will not be available from JSAS. However, the service has increased the general availability of the better technical reports.

Searching through technical reports is a waste of time for some areas of research. However, if you are working in an area supported by a major government agency, the technical report is a valuable source of information. Some examples of government-supported research are automobile driver safety, personnel training and selection, operator control of complex machines, and human decision making.

The Defense Documentation Center also carries out automated searches of technical reports. Similar to PASAR, this search uses key words to find relevant references. The listings are then printed and bound into a document. Unfortunately, you have to have a Defense Department contract, or know someone who does, in order to have such an automated search done.

REFERENCES

1. Garvey, W. D., & Griffith, B. C. Scientific communication: Its role in the conduct of research and creation of knowledge. *American Psychologist,* 1971, *26,* 349–362.

Sample Report*

Preference for Study Conditions

and Performance of College Students

William T. Garcia

University of Eastern California

Runninghead: Study Conditions

*The entire content of this report is fictitious.

Study Conditions

1

Abstract

College students studied for an introductory psychology course under either their preferred study condition--
silence, easy-listening music, or rock music--or under
a nonpreferred condition. The students' class scores
indicated that those students studying under their
preferred conditions had significantly better
performance. In addition, the students who studied under
the preferred condition of silence had significantly
higher scores than those who preferred either music
condition.

Preference for Study Conditions and

Performance of College Students

Cox and Randle (1975) have reported an increasing

trend among college students toward listening to

music while studying. These data have even been used to

explain the poorer academic performance of today's

college student (Bright & Harding, 1976). Such a

contention implies that students do more poorly when

studying with music, yet no direct evidence exists that

studying in the presence of music has an effect on

academic performance.

Research concerning the effect of noise on

performance could potentially indicate what effect music

might have on studying. However, Parr (1973) concluded

in a review article that noise can either improve or

degrade performance depending upon the subject's arousal

level. Since little is known about the arousal level

of a college student while studying, this research is not

very useful for the present study.

 The purpose of the experiment reported here,
then, was to determine if studying with a background
of music has an effect on academic performance compared
to studying in silence. In addition, since some
students study with music or in silence because they
prefer these conditions, while others do so because they
have no alternative (e.g., because of roommate preference),
preference for the study conditions was also included
as an independent variable.

Method

Subjects

 A total of 120 students from a single introductory
psychology class volunteered to serve as subjects.
Twenty were assigned to each of the six experimental
groups.

Apparatus

 A 10.2 m by 12.4 m room served as the study room.

Study Conditions

4

It contained 20 standard desk chairs. Music was
provided by a General Electric model 51-A stereo
record player.

Procedure

After volunteering for the experiment, all
students were asked to indicate whether they preferred
studying in silence, studying to easy-listening music,
or studying to rock music. Based upon these preferences,
20 students were assigned to each of three groups
according to their stated preference. The silence-
preferred group studied in a quiet room, the easy-
listening-preferred group studied to music selected by
three independent judges for its unobtrusiveness, and
the rock-preferred group studied to music selected by
the judges for its rock content.

Three additional groups of 20 students each were
assigned to nonpreference groups. For example, a
student who preferred silence would be randomly

Study Conditions

5

assigned to one of the music groups. Thus, the design

was a 2 x 3 factorial with two levels of preference--

preferred and nonpreferred--and three levels of

listening condition--silence, easy listening, and rock.

The students were asked to study for the psychology

class only when they were in their assigned room. The

room was available for 2 hours per day.

The measure of class performance was the total

number of points each student earned out of 150 possible.

These points resulted from three 50-question, multiple-

choice tests.

Results

The mean number of points earned by the students in

each of the six groups is shown in Table 1. A two-way

Insert Table 1 about here

---

analysis of variance was conducted on the individual

Study Conditions

6

scores.   The main effect of preference was found to be
significant, $\underline{F}(1, 114) = 5.7$, $\underline{p} < .05$.   The only other
effect reaching significance was the Preference x
Listening condition interaction, $\underline{F}(2, 114) = 4.8$,
$\underline{p} < .05$.

Discussion

The results support the proposition that college
students do best in a course when they are allowed
to study under preferred conditions.   As shown in Table 1
and supported by the analysis, students who studied
under preferred conditions scored significantly more
points in the course than those who studied under
nonpreferred conditions.   In addition, the significant
interaction indicates that the listening condition had
a larger effect on the students preferring their
study conditions, and since the easy-listening and
rock-preferring groups earned the same average score,
the effect must be due to the superior performance of
the silence group.

Study Conditions

7

One cannot conclude from the preferring-group data that the listening condition caused the differences in performance. It is entirely possible that those students who preferred silence were better students to begin with. Thus, the conclusion must be more specific: those students who prefer to study in silence and do so perform better in introductory psychology than do students who study under preferred conditions of easy listening or rock music.

Study Conditions

8

References

Bright, U. R., & Harding, B. G.   The declining
    performance of college students.   <u>Journal of
    Higher Education</u>, 1976, <u>14</u>, 335-341.

Cox, L., & Randle, P. R.   Listening habits of students.
    <u>Southwestern Journal of Education</u>, 1975, <u>6</u>, 272-277.

Parr, J. R.   Noise pros and cons.   <u>Review of Psychology</u>,
    1973, <u>41</u>, 18-42.

Table 1

Average Points Earned

(Total Possible 150)

Preference	Listening Condition		
	Silence	Easy Listening	Rock
Preferring	121	111	111
Nonpreferring	108	104	105

Index